THE
FRAGILE
ISLANDS

A JOURNEY THROUGH
THE OUTER HEBRIDES

For Catherine, Anna and Jonathan
with whom I first saw the
Fragile Islands.

THE
FRAGILE
ISLANDS

A JOURNEY THROUGH
THE OUTER HEBRIDES

Bettina Selby

Richard Drew Publishing
Glasgow

First published 1989 by
Richard Drew Publishing Ltd
6 Clairmont Gardens, Glasgow G3 7LW
Scotland

British Library Cataloguing in Publication Data

Selby, Bettina
    The fragile islands: a journey through the Outer Hebrides
    1. Scotland. Western Isles. Description & travel
    I. Title
    914.11'404858

    ISBN 0-86267-249-X

Printed and bound in Great Britain by
Butler and Tanner Ltd, Frome, Somerset

FOREWORD

IT WAS THE EVENING OF THE SIXTH DAY and God had finished His great work of creation and was preparing to spend the seventh day in rest when He discovered that the most precious fragments, which He had been keeping until last were still lying around in Heaven. Anxious not to have anything left undone as a temptation to Sabbath breaking, He flung the remaining pieces out at random. Sparkling like jewels they sped through space and plunged sizzling into the ice-cold sea off the north-western corner of Great Britain. Here in the few moments remaining to them before the awfulness of The First Sabbath would render all and every movement a great sin, they shuffled their small and irregular shapes into a rough chain, like a primitive necklace and became fixed forever as the Outer Hebrides, a marvellous but fragile world on the edge of a wild ocean.

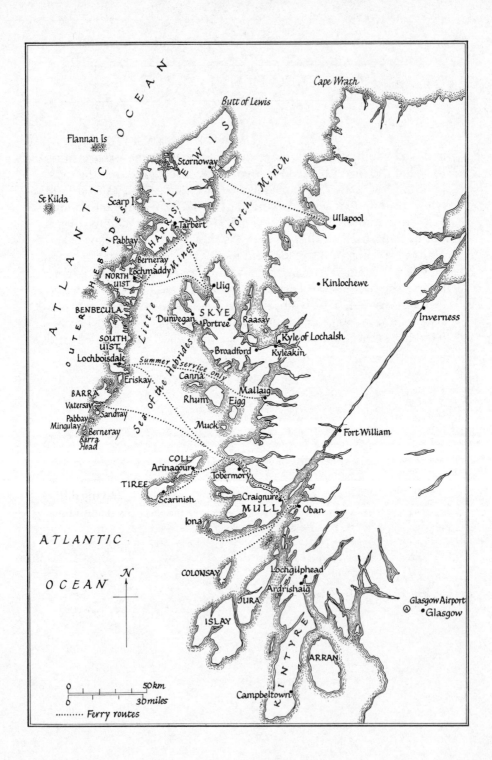

ATLANTIC OCEAN

Cape Wrath

Butt of Lewis

Flannan Is

Stornoway

North Minch

St Kilda

Scarp I

Ullapool

Tarbert

HARRIS

Pabbay

LEWIS

Berneray

Lochmaddy

NORTH UIST

Little Minch

Kinlochewe

Uig

SKYE

Dunvegan

Portree

Raasay

Inverness

BENBECULA

SOUTH UIST

Kyle of Lochalsh

Kyleakin

Broadford

Lochboisdale

Summer Hebrides service only

Eriskay

Canna

BARRA

Vatersay

Sandray

Rhum

Eigg

Mallaig

Pabbay

Mingulay

Berneray

Barra Head

Sea of the Hebrides

Muck

Fort William

COLL

Arinagour

Tobermory

TIREE

Scarinish

Craignure

MULL

Oban

Iona

ATLANTIC

OCEAN

N

COLONSAY

Lochgilphead

Ardrishaig

Glasgow Airport

Glasgow

JURA

ISLAY

KINTYRE

ARRAN

0   50 km

0   30 miles

.... Ferry routes

Campbeltown

* 8 *

ONE

. . . They gave her prow to the sea and her stern to the shore,
They hoisted up the speckled, flapping bare-topped sails,
The sea plunging and surging,
The red sea, the blue sea lashing,
And striking thither and thither about her planks.

8th Century Saga, Highland oral version

I WAS THINKING HARD ABOUT THE
legend of the last-minute making of the Outer Hebrides while I sat
in the ladies room of the island car ferry. This was really a desperate
but vain attempt to direct attention away from my queasy stomach.
The Claymore, was four hours out from Oban, bound for Barra,
with a nasty north wind whipping up the waters of the Minch into
short, steep waves which had the ship pitching and bucking with a
most unpleasant motion. There is no condition like sea-sickness for
destroying enthusiasm in anything at all and in my desire for the torture to end, or failing that, for death to intervene, I was having difficulty in retaining my interest in the prospect before me, of spending
the next few months on this afterthought of God's creation.

I had always been captivated by the Outer Hebrides since my first
visit there twenty years earlier, though this had not happened quite
immediately. I had landed towards the northern end of the chain, on
Harris and it could just as well have been the moon as I first saw it.
For it appeared entirely lunar — a dead land of dark grey rock,
devoid of vegetation, fantastically riven and fissured, brooding
sullenly under a grey, rain-swollen sky. A meaningless jumble it
seemed, of great, shapeless mounds of waste stone — more like
God's slag heap than His treasure trove. Surely no life could possibly
exist in such a desolation; the small, black-clothed, flat-capped
figures who turned their backs on the bus as it passed and scurried

away along barely perceptible paths were probably figments of my shocked imagination.

Then the bus had rounded a headland of the deeply indented coastline and the scene had changed completely. A great expanse of white shell sand stretched away into the distance, beside a sea turned suddenly into brilliant turquoise by the sun emerging from the clouds. Behind the beach was a line of steep-sided sand dunes, bound together with waving marram grass. Beyond that, level green turf, starred over with wild flowers spread out towards distant blue hills. Both the sea and the beach seemed endless and both were as pristine and as devoid of people as at the dawn of time. There was a clear rounded light everywhere as though objects were lit as much from within themselves as from an outer source. Everything shone, every pebble and every crest of every wave. The sand glistened and the birds radiated light as they plummetted into the sea or stalked the tide line. It was an entirely shimmering, shining world; at once scarcely credible and yet somehow instantly recognized. There was a quality there that was not possible to define but only to respond to. It seemed to me at that moment that I was looking at something that was as close to perfection as it was possible to come.

Over the years I visited the Outer Hebrides perhaps half a dozen times, spending just a week or so on each occasion and always finding something new and delightful that whetted my appetite to return. It became the place I dreamed about retiring to when city pavements no longer held any charm, the perfect bolt hole. Not that all my experiences on the islands were unalloyed pleasure. There were times when I would gladly have been elsewhere — when rain and wind had made a soggy misery of my tent or when damp, windless days brought out the ferocious biting midges. These minute insects sometimes descended in such dense clouds that they covered everything in sight with a blanket of unbearable irritation which drove even the locals desperate. None of these disadvantages however could quite overcome the marvellous elusive quality, that feeling of perfection which had so impressed me on the first visit and it was that which drew me to make the long journey north whenever the opportunity arose.

The native islanders themselves seemed as fascinating as their lands. They spoke among themselves in a soft-sounding archaic Gaelic language and worked at age-old pursuits, with tools that hadn't changed in centuries. Their pace of life was quite different to anything I knew, haste being entirely foreign to their natures. They were extraordinarily hospitable to strangers and never passed any-one without a greeting. But what was also becoming only too appar-ent during my latter visits was how quickly this unique life style was eroding under the pressures of the last quarter of the 20th century.

The same changes were also at work in the landscape as E.E.C. grants began to provide the sort of amenities and standardised life-style that could be found anywhere. The low, turf-thatched, stone houses that fitted naturally into their surroundings were fast being replaced by grey, prefabricated buildings of an obtrusive, box-like uniformity. Oil exploration was in full swing in the Hebridean Seas and it seemed that it could not be long before the delicate balance of nature would be destroyed as it had been on nearly every other part of Britain's coast and the Outer Hebrides as I had first seen them would be gone forever. If I was to have a deeper understanding of the unique qualities of these lovely islands before they entirely dis-appeared under the spread of concrete and convenience living, it would have to be soon.

The opportunity came in the late Spring of 1985 (which was to be followed by the wettest summer so far on record). I had just finished the project I was currently working on and had several months stretching out before me, free of any commitments. It was the ideal time of year for a Hebridean journey, just as the wild flowers of the machair were at their best and the midge season was still a long way off. So although my bank balance would have been better served by a spell of profitable employment, I packed my camping gear, loaded up the bicycle and set off to spend an island summer on these thinly covered scraps of rock, perched on the edge of the vastness of the Atlantic Ocean.

Which was why, thirty-six hours later, I was suffering torment on the MacBraynes Car Ferry, on a day when the stomachs of all but the most cast-iron of constitutions were churning around, in sympathy with the Minch. Most of the passengers were islanders, either returning from shopping trips to Oban; visits to relatives and cattle sales on other islands, or going home for a holiday from their main-land jobs. For few of them, except the youngest children was the boat trip anything of a novelty, sea is a more natural passageway for island folk than a strip of tarmac. As soon as they had come aboard they had made for shelter, settling themselves into positions of the maximum degree of comfort, away from draughts, the women and children in the saloon and the men in the bar. It was interesting to see how many of the younger women now wore trousers, something that would have been unthinkable a few years ago. The teenagers were dressed much the same as teenagers anywhere in Britain, a few months behind current fashions possibly but no more; some of the lads even sported a single earring. It was an altogether more cosmopolitan looking gathering of islanders than I ever remembered seeing on MacBraynes.

The clothing of most of the tourists on the other hand seemed not to have changed in decades — the same uniform of vibram-soled boots with trousers tucked into thick woollen socks; woolly bobble hats and long nylon cagoules. The tourists hadn't sought seats in the stuffy saloons, being far too intrigued with the unfamiliar sea sights and the excitement of the journey. Instead they had lined the rails and strolled about the decks until the misery of seasickness had overcome their interest in the scenery. Now for the most part they huddled miserably in any shelter they could find out of the wind, keeping well away from the strong smell of frying sausages and fish and chips which wafted out from the dining saloon where high tea was being served.

Between bouts of sickness I staggered to the purser's office to buy my ticket and was as usual shocked at the increase in the fares since my last visit.

'Yes it's a hundred per cent in three years and going up all the time.'

My thoughts were echoed by an elderly lady also purchasing a ticket. 'You know the motto of this company is "MacBraynes for the Highlands"' she continued. 'But everyone up here changes it to "The Highlands for MacBraynes". No competition you see; they just charge what they like. It's even worse with freight, it makes the price of food quite ridiculous.' From her accent alone, which was a product of the home counties, I could tell she wasn't an islander. She was small and thin, and rather like a bird in the quick way she moved and held her head. Her face was something like a bird's too, with sharp-pointed features and bright, inquisitive eyes. She was dressed in old, well-cut tweeds and she did not appear to be suffering from sea-sickness. I asked her if she was visiting Barra. 'No I live there,' she said. 'I'm a White Settler.' Seeing my puzzlement, she added, 'It's what the natives call incomers, I've a house on Barra and live there most of the time. Come and see me when you're passing.'

This was my first meeting with Thetis the last member of a once great English Catholic family, who now lived frugally in a small croft house on the rocky East coast of Barra. Through her mother's line she was a direct descendant of the piratical chiefs of those parts — the MacNeils of Barra and on closer acquaintance I found that she had inherited much of the spirit and tenacity of her forebears and like them she had resisted various attempts to dislodge her from her island home. She had inherited some of their humour too — one pirate ancestor had been captured and brought before that humour less King James the Sixth of Scotland before he became James the First of England. On being asked by that monarch why he had been harrying English ships, he had replied that he thought he was doing James a favour by plaguing the women who had beheaded his mother, Mary Queen of Scots.

My stomach having called a truce, I returned to the after deck, to the conversation I had been having with two tourists which had been interrupted. One of them was called Connel and came from Northern Ireland where he earned his living as a lawyer and endeavoured to keep himself and his family sane through the troubles in that unquiet country by engaging in as many outdoor pursuits as he could. Every so often he said, he just had to get right away from Ireland on his own. Like me, he found cycling an excellent antidote to the pressures of the twentieth century and was planning a five-day ride up to Stornoway, in the north-east of Lewis, from where he would catch another ferry to the mainland and ride back down south along the coast, camping out each night and returning home 'refreshed for the fray'.

'I've been doing it twice a year, for five years now,' said Connel. 'Puts me right every time. My wife thinks I'm mad. We've lovely enough country back home in Ireland, she says, why can't I ride there?'

He was about forty, trim and fit looking, dressed in the distinctive and faintly comical costume of the serious cyclist — skin-fitting, brightly-coloured, long top, with a row of pockets at the back, bulging with spare tyres and sustaining food, like a reversed marsupial pouch; skin-fitting black dancer tights and flat black shoes. The shoes are responsible for a good measure of the comic effect, as they have metal plates on the soles for engaging the pedals firmly, and off the bicycle these plates make their wearers walk about on their heels, stiff-kneed and leaning their upper torso forward to compensate, like arthritic ducks.

'She's right enough in one way,' continued Connel. 'There is wonderful countryside in Ireland, none better, but it's different out here, it's the peace, it's like another world altogether. I find it difficult to believe that bombs even exist when I'm on those islands, leave alone that people are throwing them around at one another.'

I felt a comradeship with Connel, not just for the enthusiasms we shared, but for our present sufferings too; for although he was a keen and experienced yachtsman, he had like me fallen victim to the unpleasant motion of the boat and was now looking pale and shivery. We had both struggled hard against the threatening nausea but had been finally defeated when some other stricken soul had emptied his beer mug over the side, whereupon, the contents, after lazily curling around a few times in the complex air currents, had returned on an upward eddy and already smelling stale, had splattered sickeningly all over us. It seemed sad to finally succumb after holding out for so long and with just one more hour to endure.

The other man was called Mike. He was younger than Connel and was recently divorced after a harrowing two years of trying to make his marriage work. He had told his story as though he didn't quite believe it all himself yet and was still trying to come to terms with the loss of his two small boys and all that had motivated his life for the last seven or so years. He had the air of someone waking up from a bad dream and was enjoying the journey with a boyish enthusiasm. It was his first visit to the islands he told us, although he had wanted to come to Barra for years, ever since he had seen the film of Compton MacKenzie's *Whisky Galore*. Camping there for a week was to be a much needed break, before he started rebuilding his life. He seemed to me a caring, dependable sort of person and so he proved a few days later when he struggled for hours down a rough Barra hillside, with me having badly damaged my foot draped over his shoulder.

Mike had grown visibly more relaxed as the ship had plunged and rolled its way further and further from the mainland and he'd begun to forget the preoccupations of the last few months in enjoyment of the stupendous scenery. His excitement and delight had communicated itself even through the pangs of sea-sickness and brought back memories of the first time I had sailed to Barra. That had been on an entirely different sort of day, one of heat and stillness, with the sea so flat and glass-like that the ship was reflected in it. Great shoals of basking sharks had lain about on the surface, immobile in the heat, their hugeness unbelievable and exciting. The sky had been full of birds, especially gannets looking so dazzlingly white that all the other birds were grey in comparison. We had steamed past the endless islands of the Inner Hebrides, each with its own unique and improbable outline. The great scurr of Eigg, like the prow of a marooned giant liner; Rhum's perfect cone-shaped peaks and the high, dragon-toothed cliffs of the Black Cuillin of Skye had all stood out perfectly in their turn and had slowly faded as the long thin line of the Outer Hebrides had begun to emerge from the sea, as ephemeral and insubstantial as thistledown. The heat and stillness had given the scene a highly surrealistic and improbable quality, as though it was taking place in a Celtic legend. It was like a stage set for sea creatures and birds to suddenly metamorphose into princes and princesses, after serving their three hundred years under evil enchantments; or for the seas to part and reveal drowned worlds of vanished races.

This day in contrast was cold and bright, with a sharp edge to the light and the birds were tossed about between torn rags of cloud. It was an exhilarating day but not one that was easy to enjoy in the aftermath of seasickness and I was thankful when the ship steamed into the sheltered waters of Castlebay, with the squat MacNeil castle on its small island guarding the final approach to Barra, and the more homely land scents beginning to replace the all-pervading salt smell of the sea. The castle showed no signs of life, the present chief, an American living in New York, is an absentee landlord. In previous centuries we would have arrived at the right hour to hear the traditional boast from the ramparts 'The MacNeil has dined, the rest of the world may now take its dinner'. Another month or so and Prince Charles and Princess Diana would be lunching there when they made a brief tour of this far corner of their future realm. Already I had been told of the forthcoming event at least a dozen times on the boat by returning Barra folk. They talked about it in tones of feigned indifference, referring to the prince and princess as 'the Royals' but excitement and pride bubbled away under the surface. American MacNeils on whirlwind package tours 'searching out their roots' were smug as though the royal couple were visiting their family home, as indeed they were by ancient notions of clan solidarity.

The unloading was a tame affair compared with my first visit. That was before television had reached the isles and every able bodied person — man, woman, child and babe in arms had gathered at the jetty to enjoy the main entertainment of the week, even though the ferry hadn't arrived until well after midnight. Where there was now a drive-on ferry, there had been only crane unloading then and whether the operator was less than sober, or the cables past their best, goods to be unshipped ran far more than the usual range of hazards. I'd seen one brand new motor car dropped with such abandon onto the quay that it had to be immediately craned back aboard and returned to its makers. Split packing cases and burst bales had been far more numerous than whole ones.

In spite of the modern rival attraction, a fair sprinkling of people were about on this raw May evening to meet their relatives off the boat and even more were around awaiting the arrival of food supplies, especially bread, from Oban. There was never enough bread ordered (Scottish frugality?) so shopkeepers were there to collect the fresh supply and housewives were there waiting for the shopkeepers to open shop, and sell it to them straightaway, even though it was ten o'clock at night. By the next day there would be a shortage again. It all seemed very charming and haphazard — as long as one wasn't running short of bread oneself.

Connel stayed on the boat which was continuing to the next island, South Uist, from where he would begin his cycle ride. Mike and I waved him off and then set out in the gathering dusk to make camp. We were both happy to have companionship on our first sortie into the interior and had settled beforehand on our camp site, I, because I remembered it from previous visits and Mike because he had studied his map and could see what an ideal spot there was beside the small freshwater loch which would supply drinking and washing water and which was sheltered by a raised storm beach from a fine curving bay, which looked westward over the endless ocean.

By the time we had reached the gate that led through the fields to the loch and made a courtesy call on the crofter to ask permission to camp, it was nearly midnight and almost dark and as cold as I had ever known it for May. A raw unseasonable wind was blowing from the north east making Mike's tent very difficult to pitch. The light sandy soil took the tent pegs easily but they pulled out again with equal facility until we found heavy stones to hold them down. I hadn't brought a tent, relying on a Goretex bivvy bag to keep off light showers. I much prefer this method of camping, because I can watch the stars before drifting off to sleep. It always seems a pity not to enjoy the night sky to the full on the rare occasions when the view of it isn't ruined by the sodium and neon lighting which extends every year over ever increasing tracts of countryside. In this particular summer however, it was seldom going to be possible to camp out without a tent of proven dependability, such as the one I had left at home. I decided to send for this as soon as the Post Office opened in the morning; in the meantime I accepted Mike's kind offer of hospitality and moved into his roomy tent. Fully clothed and in both my down sleeping bag and the bivvy bag it was only just warm enough.

All night long, as the canvas walls flogged and shivered, scores of birds flew in, calling as they came, for the tiny loch was the calling point of many migratory species making the great ocean crossing and late-comers for the breeding season were in a hurry to get to their nesting sites. Every time I looked out through the tent flaps, a large mute swan was sailing like a galleon down a swathe of moonlight, while the terns flitted and screamed overhead. The female swan was brooding a clutch of eggs, sitting motionless on a large rough nest of twigs and debris, raised high up out of the water, among the reeds at the far side of the loch. Everything was silvered over with the moonlight and so beautiful it seemed a waste to think of sleep.

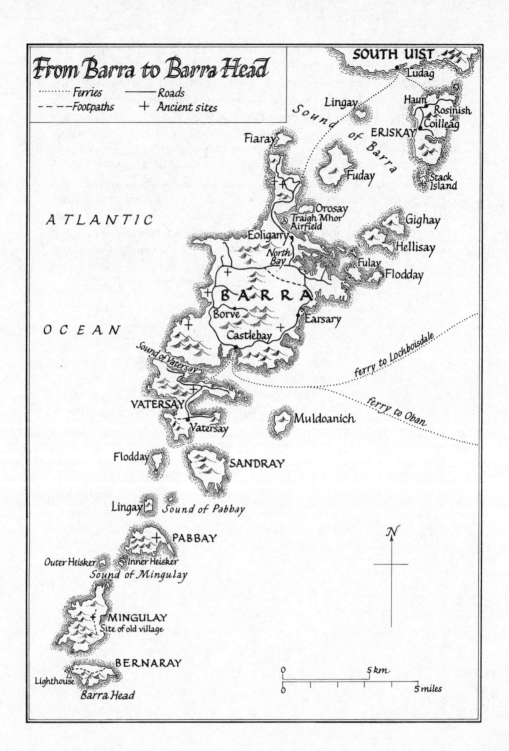

From Barra to Barra Head

Ferries .... Roads ————
Footpaths ─ ─ ─ Ancient sites +

SOUTH UIST

Ludag

Lingay

Haun

Rosinish

Coilleag

ERISKAY

Sound of Barra

Fiaray

Fuday

Stack Island

Gighay

ATLANTIC

Orosay

Traigh Mhor Airfield

Eoligarry

North Bay

Hellisay

Fulay

Floddday

OCEAN

BARRA

Borve

Earsary

Castlebay

ferry to Lochboisdale

Sound of Vatersay

VATERSAY

Vatersay

Muldoanich

ferry to Oban

Floddday

SANDRAY

Lingay

Sound of Pabbay

N

PABBAY

Outer Heisker

Inner Heisker

Sound of Mingulay

MINGULAY
Site of old village

BERNARAY

Lighthouse

Barra Head

0 ————————— 5 km
0 ————————— 5 miles

This island of Barray lies about two leagues and a half
to the south-west of South-Uist; it is five miles in
length and three in breadth. . . . There are several old
forts to be seen here and there is a great plenty of fish.

Martin Martin 1703

THE SPOT WE HAD CHOSEN TO PITCH
the tent was very good as we discovered in the full light of morning.
Apart from the obvious attractions of the views and the fresh water,
it was also sheltered to the rear by a low rocky bluff that had the
added advantage of containing a number of shallow nooks and hollows for storing food and equipment and for keeping rain off cooking gear and firewood. With a few additional rocks and washed up
fish boxes strategically arranged to serve as fireplace, seats and table
we had the sort of outdoor domestic arrangement that was little
short of perfection. Mike liked it so well he decided to spend his
whole week camped there, while I proposed to stay for just a night
or two, before setting out on my bicycle to explore the island
thoroughly. As it happened circumstances kept me by the small
loch for nearly a month and at the end of that time I still thought it
was one of the best camp sites I had ever had.

Half a mile away, across the white horseshoe of Hallaman Bay
sands, but hidden from immediate view by the bluff, a starkly modern hotel stood out in sharp-edged detail against the shaggy hills
behind it. It was new since my last visit and apart from its unsympa-
thetic design, was a welcome asset, providing a bar for locals and
casuals, as well as twentieth century comfort at moderate cost.
Somewhere to visit for the occasional drink and a meal off a china
plate makes a considerable difference to the pleasure of camping,

especially when the weather is cold or wet. Such places are rare in the Outer Isles and this one had been built at a vast cost by the Highland and Island Development Board about five years earlier. Finding that it lost money at a spectacular rate it had been sold off cheaply to a local man who was also given a substantial grant to refurbish it. This man already owned one hotel in Castlebay and another small one at Northbay and it seemed he had more idea than the Development Board of how to make it pay. His method was simply to make it as easy as possible for people to visit by offering an all-in package which included travel and trips around the island. It was nearly always full while I was on Barra, mainly with successive parties of the 'root-finding' American descendants of Barra folk expelled in the notorious 'clearances' of the 19th century. These people all shared a marked resemblance to one another, as though they had stayed together and intermarried throughout the generations of their exile. They were notable for their low stature combined with considerable girth, most of which was tightly encased in very bright tartan. They were carefully protected from the elements by being whisked around the island in a coach and as they spent only a night or so on Barra, they left again with their illusions unshattered — it had been exactly as they had expected it would be 'Just too quaint for words'.

It was at the back of the hill that sheltered the loch from south-westerly winds that I did the damage to my foot, which resulted in my prolonged stay on Barra. A wild, boggy area slopes down on the seaward side of the hill to precipitous sea-cliffs, loud with the clamour of nesting gulls. Perched on a conspicuous, overhanging promontory of the cliffs is a pile of roughly hewn, crumbling stones, the remains of an ancient watch tower. With my eye on this mouldering heap, instead of on the treacherous footing, I jumped down from a fence and landed with a searing pain and a sickening sound of something snapping as my foot doubled up under me at an ominously acute angle.

It transpired that I hadn't broken a bone but had instead torn several ligaments and tendons. This sort of injury can be a lot more trouble than a simple fracture, being difficult to diagnose, and often taking longer to heal. At first it had seemed — apart from the pain — that the damage was minimal and it wasn't until I returned to the surgeon, for a check-up, ten days after the accident that the extent of the damage was fully apparent. He then put the leg in a plaster cast from the toes to the knee and I was much more comfortable and able to get about again, for I found to my delight that I could ride my bicycle quite well in plaster, whereas it had been impossible with the ankle unsupported. It was a great improvement on the slow, painful and tiring business of swinging along on crutches.

On its positive side, the accident afforded me an inside view into the working of the Health Service in these outlying parts, where I thought there were distinct advantages over the service that exists in many of our large cities. There were no lengthy waiting lists and the attention, once one reached the hospital was prompt and friendly. However, as there were no X-ray facilities on Barra it meant an involved journey to the hospital at Daliburgh on South Uist, the next island to the north.

A local passenger ferry plies across the Sound of Barra, and an ambulance was summoned to take me to the jetty. To my surprise I recognised the driver as the owner of one of Castlebay's five grocery shops and proprietor of the only petrol pump on the island. He had impressed himself indelibly on my memory the previous day when I had fished out a discarded can of oil from the waste bin at the side of the pump. In order to prevent corrosion, cycle chains need small amounts of oil to be applied very frequently in damp, seaside areas. The residue left in a can after a motorist has topped up his sump is more than enough for the purpose. In all the years I had availed myself of this free source of lubrication, this same ambulance driver was the only person who found fault with me over the practice.

'Could ye no afford to buy one?' he'd yelled at me from the door-way of his shop opposite. I'd thought he was making a joke and had tossed back some pleasantry or other, only to realise from the expression on his face and the truculent angle of his chin that he was in deadly earnest.

'It had been thrown away; it was an empty tin,' I said defensively.

'If it was empty ye'd not be wanting it,' he'd replied triumphantly.

He was all smiles as he loaded me into the ambulance however and even seemed pleased to see me. It transpired that he owned the vehicle and was on contract to the Health Service and so today I was providing welcome business. I was sore about being publicly harangued the day before and once we were under way I took the opportunity to explain why it was more convenient to use dis-carded oil rather than risk carrying a supply which always tends to leak and seep into other items in the pannier bags. He dismissed the matter with an airy wave of his hand.

'I'm no the man to begrudge a wee bitty oil to any customer of mine,' he said magnanimously. From which I gathered that I had now earned the privilege of making use of his oil empties.

Six miles of water separates Barra from the southern shores of South Uist. Innumerable rocks and small islets intervene as well as the larger islands of Fuday, Lingay and Eriskay. Dangerous waters for any craft, where for only two short periods a day is the tide right for the ferry crossing and even then the amount of leeway between certain rocks and over perilous shallows can be measured in inches. It was in these waters that the S.S. Politician went down in the last war, having made a very small error in her navigation. She was carrying a cargo of prestigious British goods to America, mostly fine Scotch whisky. The subsequent looting of this cargo by the islanders was the subject of Compton Mackenzie's hilariously funny book *Whisky Galore.* What he wrote was no more than a factual account of the proceedings according to many of the islanders I met, whose fathers and uncles had taken part in the salvage and in the battles of hide-and-seek with the Customs and Excise officers which had followed.

When we arrived at the jetty it was between ferry times and the ferryman, summoned in advance by radio was waiting with a dinghy to get us aboard. It was still possible to cross by following a tortuous roundabout route, which only someone familiar with these parts since childhood could hope to follow. The hour long boat trip was Mike's reward for gallantly insisting on accompanying me when I had thought he should stay on Barra and enjoy his interrupted walk. The day had turned into one of warm blue skies so that we could sit on deck, soaking up the sunshine and making the most of the changing vistas of sea, sky and rock.

'And all free and paid for by Maggie Thatcher today — seeing as how you're injured,' said the ferryman.

The normal route on a fine day, takes about forty minutes and is full of beauty and interest, but this circuitous way was even lovelier because the wild life, normally undisturbed was far more abundant. Rows of oily, green-tinged, black shags stood on rocks, heads bent forward, peering intently into the sea, waiting an opportunity to plunge in after a fish. In marked contrast solitary, white, shining gannets fell from the sky in their plummetting, heart-stopping dive. Occasional herons, stately and motionless, poised over rock pools on one long, slender leg. Most thrilling of all were the Atlantic grey seals lying out sunbathing on the bare rock skerries in small groups. In the water they look very dark but there is often a pattern, like marbling, clearly visible on their sun-dried fur and never the same on any two coats. Their colour varies greatly too, from dark gun-metal to palest dove-grey. Occasionally one would scratch its stomach luxuriously with a beautiful hand-like flipper and yawn and grunt contentedly, while settling into a more comfortable position. If the boat came too close they became alarmed and slid into the water, with what looked like reproachful glances from their huge, human-looking brown eyes. There is much about seals which appears very human and accounts for the Scottish 'Selkie' legends where they are attributed with both a land and a sea existence and the doubtful, two-edged gift of sharing in the life of men. There are many such tales as the one of a mariner callously striking at a great bull seal with his oar and wounding the creature on its head; later he lands on an island where he is met by a hermit with a deep gash down the side of his face and the mariner realises what he had done with his wanton action. After years of seeing seal heads suddenly breaking surface close by, my first thought is still that I'm encountering a bald-headed man out for a swim. Best of all is to watch them from the top of remote island cliffs when they are riding the foam of wild Atlantic water, sporting in the crashing breakers with a freedom and ease that looks like pure enjoyment and is difficult not to envy.

The ambulance which was awaiting us by the Ludag jetty was part of the regular ambulance service and very different from our relaxed Barra transport. It was driven by a stout man in a grey ambulance uniform instead of the ubiquitous blue overalls worn by all grown island males. He was very punctilious about regulations and much to the ferryman's scorn he'd parked his ambulance quite a way from where we moored at the foot of the jetty.

'It's that Englishman you've got, worse luck for you,' said the ferryman as we drew near. Aloud he called, 'The lassie's hurt her foot, can ye no bring the ambulance down'?

The driver didn't answer but when he was holding my arm to help me hop the hundred yards to where he'd parked, he said, 'There's great waves can break over that jetty in the gales, it's right dangerous, so we're not allowed to take the ambulance down.'

It wasn't the sort of statement that invited a reply, anyway I needed all my breath for the violent exercise: a hundred yards is a long way to hop. Inside the ambulance, he strapped both Mike and myself into our seat belts, as though we were small children.

'It's a terrible road till we get near to Daliburgh, so don't think you'll be comfortable,' he said with an air of satisfaction. He took a rather truculent tone with us I thought, which was not improved by our refusal to agree with his low opinion of the Barra ambulance with which he clearly felt himself in competition. We decided eventually that it was just his blunt Yorkshire manner coupled with the fact that having married a local girl and lived up here for twenty years, he seemed to feel that he was still treated as a stranger. He wasn't the first incomer to express this sentiment and I think in each case that it had a great deal to do with not having managed to learn Gaelic, which is still the first language of most people in the Western Isles.

The hospital was quite delightful, the sort of place one would choose to be ill in if one could. Small and friendly, it didn't even have the usual antiseptic hospital smell. Originally it had been run by a Roman Catholic nursing order and had a life-sized, dazzling white statue of Jesus in the front drive and the name over the entrance was the Hospital of the Sacred Heart.

'Not now though, it's called Daliburgh Hospital now,' our driver had said. 'It's not Catholic anymore, whatever anybody tells you and all our doctors are black, one from India, one from Pakistan and one from Africa. It's Dr. Moses you'll be seeing, he's the one from India.' He watched us closely in his driving mirror, to see, we thought, if we would express any racist sentiment. 'He's a born again Christian,' he added, 'which is why he changed his name to Moses. He's very good and he'll stand no nonsense; if he says you stay the night, that's it, you'll stay.'

Mr. Moses was not at all the moralising chauvinist I had rather expected from the driver's description. He was a charming urbane man who seemed delighted that I had travelled in India and we exchanged views on places we both knew. There was no-one else waiting for attention, indeed there seemed to be no patients at all staying in the hospital and a pleasant air of leisure prevailed, quite unlike that of any other hospital I've ever visited. I was intrigued to discover how he found life on this wind-swept scrap of northern land, after the heat and colour and bustle of India. He said that he was still enjoying the contrast very much, both in life and work. There weren't the same problems of corruption over here nor the vast difference between public and private health care which he said was the case in India and of which even I as a casual visitor had been aware. The disadvantages of being a general surgeon in The Western Isles, he thought were that you were involved in only minor problems; anything serious was immediately flown to the mainland.

His wife, who came in to meet me said that she thought the main disadvantage in living on the Outer Hebrides was the weather and she didn't think she had ever been warm since she came there. She was glad to have seen it, but home was home and she would be happy to be back among her own people.

After being X-rayed, bandaged, supplied with crutches and given some much needed refreshment — the first we'd had in seven hours, we were hurried back to the jetty in the other ambulance, whose driver had no inhibitions about driving right to the end of the pier to load us, just in time, on to the evening ferry run. We were back in camp fourteen hours after we had left it that morning. I was an hour later than Mike because it took me that long to get across Hallaman Bay with my crutches sinking deep into the sand at every step.

I gained a closer acquaintance with the swans over the next few days, as I lay about outside the tent and after the first day, the female no longer left her nest as I came down to the loch to steep my foot in the cold water (Mr. Moses had recommended ice-packs and this seemed a close approximation). The male swan was useless at defending his mate and whenever real or imagined danger threatened he just turned his back and swam off. I wondered if this had anything to do with his previous encounters with humans, for breeding cobs are normally quite aggressive. Someone had at some time ringed him with a thick circlet of plastic material around his neck, which moved up to his head when he bent to graze below the water and sank again to the base of his neck when he raised his head. I resented this obtrusive marring of his beauty and thought it might have affected his instincts. He took an occasional turn on the nest for very short periods while the pen grazed, and towards the end of the incubation period he began making short flights across the loch, with tremendous beating of wing tips against the surface of the water and straining forward of his long serpentine neck in the immense effort to get the heavy body airborne. The impression of power he conveyed was awe-inspiring. Sometimes wild geese also flew low over the loch but the swan's flight was infinitely more arresting.

Greater black backed gulls, of which there were several pairs nesting behind the hill, also kept a watchful eye on the swan's nest. I find it difficult to like these large ungainly bullies, with their loud, unmusical squawking. They keep up a ceaseless patrol of other birds' nests, for they are avian terrorists, perpetually alert to snatch any fledgling that is left for a moment unguarded. Their chilling vigilance yields them rich rewards and they did eventually get one of the cygnets, for when, one thrilling morning, seven exquisite balls of pale grey fluff accompanied the two proud parents moving in slow, stately splendour across the loch, one of the babies seemed to be losing contact with the flotilla. The parent swans were at first very aware and kept shepherding the youngster back to the protection of the group, but it soon became apparent that the cygnet was blind and could keep in touch only by hearing and these swans were mute. As the day progressed the adults grew less attentive towards the stricken cygnet and he became quite separated from them, cowering in the reeds by the loch side. Towards evening he roused himself and as though he sensed the presence of his family feeding in the centre of the water, began to swim purposefully to where they were. The adults saw him and started to move swiftly towards him, perhaps aware of the danger I had not yet seen. While they were still some way off, one of the black backs swooped down with a triumphal squawk and took the blind cygnet behind the neck. He was away in the air with him in a flash, the little black feet of the cygnet moving rapidly as though it hadn't yet realised its fate and thought it was still swimming. I could only hope that its death would be swift. After this incident the swans moved all their brood to a larger loch and before I left Barra I was pleased to note that all six remaining cygnets were well and thriving.

A rival attraction to the swans was the unmistakable and exciting sound and the sudden flash of movement as a large brown trout leapt and splashed back into the water. A movement so fast and unexpected, that only the sound and the spreading concentric rings on the surface of the water confirmed the reality of it. The loch was too shallow for swimming but it was said to be the best fishing loch on the island and certainly the fish I had from it were a good size and an excellent flavour. Unfortunately we had none while Mike was there, which was a pity for he longed to catch something, no matter what so long as it was a fish and could be cooked in the open on his camp fire. He had repeatedly fished both sea and loch with no success; he couldn't even buy a fish from any of the five Castlebay shops, or from the boats in the harbour and this is the sad state of affairs in most of the islands — a fact hard to credit in a place where every second person is a fisherman.

I felt particularly sad about the lack of fish for Mike because he set so much store by it and he had been such a staunch companion to me when I was injured and never complained once afterwards about doing all the camp chores; had I been his mother he could not have looked after me more caringly. Before he left he made sure I had enough food and a good supply of driftwood and even found me a legless moulded plastic chair, washed up on the beach, which mounted on one of the fish boxes made a most comfortable seat for my enforced immobility. There was little enough I could do for him in return, except to lend a sympathetic ear while he unburdened himself of some of the bitter memories of his broken marriage. I think talking about such things to someone who will listen without too much comment can be helpful. But this small service was as nothing compared with the influence that the island itself worked. A week of living outdoors in such marvellous surroundings had resulted in an altogether happier and more relaxed young man, who was leaving Barra with energy renewed, eager to get on with his life.

With the perversity of fate, once Mike had departed, I was treated almost daily to delicious pink-fleshed trout. These were given to me by a holidaying fisherman who patiently stalked the loch with such cunning and skill that he caught far more fish than he needed. I sustained his efforts with cups of tea and coffee, whenever his casting arm needed a rest. This luxurious food supply — cooked simply by wrapping in foil and laying it on the hot embers of a driftwood fire — continued until after I had returned to the hospital, where Mr. Moses, rather shocked and very sympathetic over the unhealed foot, put it into plaster and so ended my period of inactivity.

CHAPTER
THREE

Macneil of Barra and all his followers are Roman Catholics, only one excepted, viz., Murdock Macneil; and it may be thought no small virtue in him to adhere to the Protestant communion, considering the disadvantages he labours under, by the want of his chief's favour, which is much lessened for being a heretic as they call him.

Martin Martin

THERE IS NOTHING THAT SO MUCH enhances the quality of life it seems, as being temporarily deprived of some facility or other and then having it restored. I had enjoyed the intimate association with the loch and its bird life, which the enforced period of inactivity had given me, but it had been galling too, particularly on wet days when I lay cramped and bored in my small tent. So it felt wonderfully exhilarating to be mobile again and able to explore further afield. Not that I could return immediately to full activity. Mr. Moses thought it would be several months before the foot was back to normal, but I was happy enough at this stage to extend my boundaries by just a mile or two.

Had I come equipped with a conventional bicycle I should probably not have been able to ride it with a leg in plaster, but fortunately I had been persuaded by my friends at Evans Bike Shop to make this journey on an entirely different machine, one of a type which had originated in America and was gaining great popularity over here. It was called a 'mountain', or 'all terrain' bicycle and it was intended to be ridden over rough ground and through open countryside where an ordinary bicycle would get bogged down or be likely to suffer damage. Two such bicycles, made by the same manufacturer as the one I had been offered, had recently been ridden to the top of Mt. Kilimanjaro in Africa. With such an impressive example before me, particularly as I intended getting off the beaten track and riding over rough ground, I had accepted the kind offer.

Apart from the fat, knobbly tyres, wide handlebars and chunky pedals without toe clips, the mountain bicycle had many features which made it very suitable for someone with only one sound foot. Chief amongst these was the chain wheel, or rather wheels, for there were three of them, which combined with the six cogs at the rear gave a staggering total of eighteen gears, with which it should be possible to ascend the steepest hill with the minimum of effort. I should perhaps explain for the benefit of those unfamiliar with bicycles, that a chain-wheel is the large shiny cog to which the right hand crank is attached and around which the chain is pulled as the pedals are turned (thus facilitating forward progress). A chain-wheel is usually circular, but on this mountain bicycle it was elliptical, which was very novel and strange looking, and was supposed to get over the 'dead' part of the revolution of the chain-wheel. This occurs when one foot has pushed its pedal round and the other foot hasn't quite got to the position where it can exert its maximum pressure. To my delight this theory actually worked in practice and whereas previously, when I had two good feet, I had hardly been aware of the effect, now I found I could pedal practically single footed, putting only minimal strain on the injury. The slow but inexorable progress that I made, coupled with the rough nature of the ground that could be traversed on this bicycle led me to think of it affectionately as 'Evans the Tank'.

If my camp site had been less ideal, it would have made sense at this stage to have moved the tent nearer the road, as it was no easy matter traversing the half-mile or so with my crutches tied to the cross bar of the 'Tank' and the day's supply of necessaries weighing down the panniers. In a climate where sun, rain, sleet, fog and snow can occur on the same day, these necessaries included rain gear, extra sweater, tools for the Tank, iron rations, torch, map, compass and so forth. The first part of the trek, across the close-cropped machair was not too arduous, I had only to avoid the extensive earthworks of rabbit colonies and the corpses of sheep and new born lambs which were illegally left to rot, or to be pecked clean by scavenging birds. Black-faced sheep roamed freely on the common grazing and on the road; in fact they ranged freely in every place which was not securely fenced in against them. They were always getting into people's gardens and when it rained they huddled in doorways, so that it was difficult to get out of the houses and even more difficult to avoid the piles of dung made pungently liquid by the rain. Sheep were the most ubiquitous life form of Barra, more numerous it seemed at times than the gulls. Most people who kept no sheep were outspoken in their dislike of them, saying that they had become no better than vermin. They poured scorn on a system that paid out subsidies on the number of sheep kept, rather than on the number that were brought successfully to market. It no longer made sense for a man to weed out his old unproductive ewes, they said and so these aged sheep continued to give birth to weak or still-born lambs, until they themselves dropped dead of old age, or fell into streams, from which they were too weak to clamber out. I hoped these bloated carcasses would be removed before the 'Royals' visited.

After the machair, I had a stream to cross which had cut a deep bed for itself through soft shifting sand. As long as I could get up sufficient speed, screwing up my courage to let the Tank plunge slitheringly down the steep slope, I could normally ride through the stream dry-shod. Then came the hardest part, where I had to haul myself and the laden Tank up the sandy bank on the far side of the stream. There was no way to avoid this area of soft sand, which was spreading inexorably into the fragile machair.

When I finally stood panting at the top, my efforts were rewarded by an arresting modern sculpture, quite as good I thought as many of the controversial exhibits on show in the new wing of the Tate Gallery. It was an arrangement of abandoned saloon cars of various colours and periods – an incidental memorial to the changing styles of the motor age, a sort of outdoor museum. Scoured and sand-blasted through seasons of westerly gales, it stood there looking extraordinarily alien and self-conscious, on the ribbed contours of the fine, wind-blown sand. The farmer who owned the land said that he had dragged the cars there with a tractor, not with any artis-tic pretension but in an attempt to halt the soil erosion. I thought this was a case of justification after the event, for such piles of defunct cars, buses, trucks, tractors, vans and lorries occur through-out Barra, as apart from being pushed over cliffs into the sea (and there are few accessible cliffs in Barra) there is nowhere for them to go. Whatever the intention, this particular pile of rusting metal cer-tainly wasn't helping to stop the soil erosion and the cars themselves were being gradually buried by the advancing sand. What was needed was to re-establish the marram grass which elsewhere bound the margins of the sea.

Only a few more sandy encroachments interrupted the rest of my passage up through the fields to the road. Skylarks and lapwings abounded and so did rotted, half buried fences, for which I needed to keep a wary eye open, as even Evans the Tank did not take kindly to wire strands caught in his wheels. These fences were a perfect nuisance and occurred in various states of disintegration all over the island, often in quite ridiculous sites and had been erected some time in the recent past, the result of another indiscriminate grant which paid out for fencing by the yard, without checking on its need, use or efficiency. Sheep were forever getting enmeshed in the wire and went about trailing long lengths of it (both barbed and plain) firmly embedded in their fleeces.

One single-track road circles the island, linking the villages, with side roads branching off to other habitations on the many airds and peninsulas that give Barra such an indented coastline. Having reached the road, I had the choice of going right or left. If the day was good, I turned left to follow the west coast, and continued my explorations down the little tracks, so that after circling the island I eventually reached Castlebay by evening and could buy whatever stores I needed on the way back to the tent. If the day was wet, I turned right and went straight to Castlebay to read in the library where there were some useful local history books. The library, open to the general public, was housed in the centre of a newly built school, where the pupils were constantly passing through, on their way to and from lessons. The bookcases formed secluded bays — useful cover for the older boys and girls, whose interest in the opposite sex was as single-minded as it is anywhere else. The unfolding of a romance, or, more often, the baiting of vulnerable, pimply youths by girls twice their match in wit and cunning often proved more diverting than the book I was reading.

It was quite the best designed and most luxurious state school building I had ever seen and very different to the low-cost, open-plan, shoebox-type schools, in which so many of our town children have been expected to acquire an education in the last few decades. The exterior was perhaps less sympathetic and the stern modern lines made a strange contrast with the houses round about, which for the most part were old, squat cottages, hugging the rough, uncultivated hillside in no particular order or pattern, as though they had sprung up there at random, like shaggy, worm-eaten mushrooms. It was plain that such anarchy was no longer countenanced; any house newly built was squared up with its neighbours in an orderly and entirely, un-Hebridean uniformity.

The other outstanding new edifice in this, the commercial and social centre of Barra was the Co-op, a strangely sinister building, more like an outsize container, or a missile hangar, than a shop in a prime position in the High Street. Its corrugated metal structure, flat roofed and uncompromisingly rectangular was quite devoid of any windows or alleviated by any form of decoration whatsoever. Architecture in the islands has never had much pretension to being any thing more than strictly utilitarian, but the squat cottages had at least the grace of blending into the landscape, which no-one could accuse the new Co-op of doing.

Nearer to the quay were several small hotels. The one owned by the enterprising local tycoon was in the process of being refitted and was to have all the modern benefits of sauna, jacuzzis and so forth. I hoped that it would also have the sort of bar arrangement that was such a comfort at the Hallaman Bay Hotel, as there was really nowhere in Castlebay where the casual visitor could enjoy a drink or a meal. A café serving tea and eggs on toast did open later in the summer, but on my reading days, when I felt the need of mid-morning refreshment, the only place I found it was in the tourist office which was housed in a decaying little shack, where a friendly young woman and her pre-school child helped visitors to find B&B accommodation, and made coffee behind the counter when there was a slack period.

A row of two-storey houses of an older type led down to the quay, one, the Post Office, hired out perilous bicycles many of whose vital parts were either missing or malfunctioning. Most of the other shops were general stores, selling exactly the same kind of groceries, wellington boots, fluorescent nylon socks and off-licence drinks as each other (except for the one belonging to the ambulance man who also of course had the sole and undisputed petrol pump). This was the mercantile heart of the island that seventy years ago had been the centre of a short-lived Klondike, when the herring was king and where, during the riotous, six-week fishing season, every inch of water front was packed with barrels, trestles and all the effluvia of a busy fishing port. Fisher girls came from all over Scotland, to stand shoulder to shoulder, sleeves rolled up high on brawny arms, knives flicking in and out with a practised ease, as they gutted, salted and packed the sea harvest. In those days fishing boats were so numerous in the bay, that it was said you could walk across their decks to the neighbouring island of Vatersay. Old photographs of the period show animated scenes which makes the present village seem rather like a sad abandoned ghost town in comparison. Looking at these sepia prints you can almost smell the piles of fish guts, overpowering all other scents and hear the cries and the shouts, the squawks of raiding gulls and the unending streams of banter and the songs traditional to the work. Greed killed the industry, as newer and ever more 'efficient' methods of fishing succeeded in destroying the herrings' spawning grounds.

This was the sort of information I was gleaning from my readings in the library; the fleshing out of the facts was happening too as I began to meet some of the older, local people who were prepared to talk to me about the Barra of their youth. It was a great pity they told me that 'I had not the Gaelic' and indeed it was quite apparent that they were having first to translate their memories into an alien tongue and doubtless much was lost in the process.

The person from whom I learnt most was Elizabeth. She lived on the barren, rocky east coast, in a small house that stood alone at the top of a steep little rise. I met her one day when I had alighted from Evans the Tank by her gate, in order to take in the view of the scatter of islets in the sea below. It was the first dry day after a period of rain, and sky, sea and rock all shone as though they had been scrubbed and the light had a blue transparent sheen to it. It was the sort of day when no-one could bear to stay indoors and even the cats had left the firesides and sat blinking and washing themselves on dry-stone walls. The seven miles I had covered had taken me hours because I had had to keep stopping to take in view after magnificent view until I felt almost dizzy with so much beauty.

Elizabeth was planting vegetable seed in her garden, not with any great energy, for she was well over seventy and rather stout and a heart condition made her a semi-invalid. It was more in the nature of wanting to dabble her fingers in the black soil on such a day, she said later. She was a widow, with a married son living across the Minch in Oban. He came over quite often at weekends, to tend the garden and keep the house in order, so her creature comforts were well looked after but she sorely missed company.

'Ach, I'm in no hurry at all with it,' she'd said, when I'd offered to give her a hand with the planting. 'It will still be here when I'm gone, anyway I'm sure you could do with a bit of a rest yourself.' So we'd sat in her porch and drunk tea and nibbled chocolate biscuits and she'd totally captivated me with the vividness of her early recollections, so that it was hours later before I could drag myself away. After that I visited her several times, even spending one wild stormy night, sleeping on the sofa in the 'priest's' room.

On that first occasion, she tried to tell me something of the intensity of her feelings about her island home. 'I was seven years old,' she said, 'when I first saw the machair and I thought it must be fairyland. My father had taken me in the boat to be out from under my mother's feet and when he'd rowed it round to Eoligarry, he told me to wait on the beach by the boat, while he went with my brother to fetch shells from the other side, for making lime. But when I looked up and I saw the lovely green grass stretching on and on, with the silver and gold flowers all over it and the big house beyond (which isn't there anymore) I could not hold myself back, I had to run and run up the hill to the top. And all the time I was worried about my father finding me gone. So back I went to the boat and I saw I'd missed him, for he'd come with a load of shells and gone back for more. I was frightened then all right at what he'd say, but even so I couldn't wait there, but back I had to run, up the hill. Oh it drew me just, it was so lovely.'

She had been born within a stone's throw of her present house, the youngest of nine surviving children. That nearly all her childhood memories are happy undoubtedly has something to do with the distance from which she looks back to them, but it must also owe a great deal to her good fortune in being born at what was the best period for the islanders since the Jacobite Rising of 1745. Some twenty years before her birth, the oppressed, exploited peasantry of the Scottish Highlands and Islands had at last been given legal recognition and granted security of tenure over the miserable plots of land which they rented from the landlords and from which, up until that time, they could be expelled without warning or redress.

The Crofting Act of 1886 changed the status of the islanders overnight and just as suddenly gave them the hope of a reasonable future, where before there had been only the prospect of bleak survival. It made sense now to try to improve the fertility of the soil; marginal though it might be and debased by centuries of mismanagement, for now it would be theirs and their children's after them, for as long as they chose to work it. The symbols of this new order were the stone houses which the crofters built to replace their old temporary turf structures. Throughout the islands I was to meet old men and women who told me proudly that they were living in the house which had been built by their father or their grandfather in the late 1880s. The houses had been much improved since they were first built, for most had started out as very simple two-roomed cottages with little in the way of conveniences, but the difference in life-style they represented to the original builders has to be seen in relation to the generations of privation and indignity which had been the lot of these people.

The newly assigned crofts were never intended or expected to supply the whole of a family's livelihood, being really nothing more than extended allotments, which, with a cow, a few chickens and maybe a sheep or two would provide most of the basic necessities of life. Paid employment of some kind was also needed to supplement the croft and as each child reached its early teens, he or she would have to leave home to find work, most usually on the mainland. Only the eldest surviving son would inherit the croft, returning from wherever he was, to take over when his parents grew too old to cope with the work. Those working away would try to send small sums of money home, especially where there were younger dependent children. It was this sort of generosity which had enabled Elizabeth to stay on at school and eventually to train as a teacher. A strong link with their homes seems to have lasted life-long and most islanders returned as often as they could, to spend their holidays working on the croft.

There was no shortage of additional work in the first two decades of the 20th century. With trade booming and British goods being shipped all over the world, the merchant navy was at its strongest and most of the Barra men joined this service. It was said that there was hardly a British merchant ship without one or two Barra men on it and no port in the world where a seaman from the islands could not find another with whom to speak Gaelic. Even today the older Barra men are keen to ask visitors where they come from and are not satisfied with answers like 'America' or 'New Zealand', but want to pinpoint the exact spot. They have such a wide, first hand knowledge of geography, and there seem to be few places that are not known to them.

There was also at this time, plenty of work in the herring fishing, and in all the many crafts concerned with boat building and repair, as well as the jobs of farrier, cooper, blacksmith, cobbler and so forth. It was not really until the following decade that the acceleration of change brought about such profound effects upon the life styles of the Western world and particularly upon this small island margin of it.

With most of the men away at sea, the daily work of the crofts was carried on by the women, which made for a self-reliant matriarchy special to Barra, for the men of the other islands did not join the merchant navy to anything like the same extent and so were able to hold on to their traditional male dominance. Children also served a useful role and in addition to working on the croft, they helped with the care of younger children. Elizabeth said she spent most of her early life in the next door house where there were younger children for her to 'practise on'. She made it all sound rather like the 'good life' expanded to embrace a whole community, with everyone a valued member and confident of their role within it, and even if three quarters of what she told me is just romantic memory, I still think that something of great worth has been lost. No-one I was told, ever went hungry at this time, if there was a poor potato harvest, there was always fish to be had, and widows and anyone else in need naturally got a share. Much of the work had to be communal — such as gathering the sheep from the hills, hauling in the boats and shrinking the finished lengths of hand-woven tweed, and all this added to the strong sense of community. On a Sunday after mass, Elizabeth would often walk, she said, right round the island with several girl friends. They could stop for refreshment every mile or so, at each village if they wanted to, for there was nowhere on Barra where there wasn't a cousin or an aunt or someone related to one or other of them.

'We thought nothing at all of walking all day then, I don't think one of us had ever been in a car. We knew every piece and parcel of Barra. There was nowhere at all we couldn't go, except where the boys were learning to swim. We'd to look the other way if we passed there because they swam in just their skin.'

One cloud in Elizabeth's memory makes sense only against this background of a close, mutually dependent community and it had to do with the presence of a handful of Protestant families in the otherwise solidly Roman Catholic island. She became aware that a few children at school were treated differently from the others (better she claimed) withdrawn from religious instruction and 'made a fuss of by the teachers' (curiously also Protestant). The reason for their presence was that the northern part of the island — Eoligarry, the fertile machair that the young Elizabeth had thought was fairyland had been sold by the impoverished Macneil of the day. The new owner was Protestant and had brought Protestant families with him from North Uist to serve as labour on his farm and servants for the house, persuading them to make the change by settling them on the richest crofts. A church was built for their worship, and a manse for their minister, which is still the finest building on the island. Not unnaturally the presence of even a handful of families who thought and acted differently, in the most important aspect of life at that time had a profound effect upon a small island community. As Elizabeth said, it wasn't that they were unpleasant children but simply that they were cut off from the rest, that they were 'different' that filled her with such sadness. She hadn't realised until then that people could be deeply divided.

The religious division of the Outer Hebrides is curious and not really like anywhere else. South of an imaginary line bisecting Benbecula, the islands are almost 100 per cent Roman Catholic, having been re-evangelised in the 18th century, after all the proscriptions following the Dissolution, Reformation and the forceful teachings of John Knox, Oliver Cromwell and other religious fire-eaters. North of the line, the situation is more complicated, as the people there, in the fiercely religious days of the 18th and 19th centuries leaned towards the new evangelical preachings rather than towards the Old Religion, with the result that now, various sects of the Scottish Church (most of them non-conformist) hold a stern Sabbatarian sway. There is the Free Church, the Free Church of Scotland and the Church of Scotland (I think there might well be more which I have failed to identify) and each of them is quite different and not at all approved of by the members of the other two. None of them of course approve of the Roman Catholics, nor of the Episcopal Church which is thought of as almost as bad, being so full of the sort of things that Oliver Cromwell was so expressly against — altar furnishings and candles, images, genuflections and all such 'damned popery'.

As far as I have been able to ascertain, there has never been the sort of religious intolerance between Protestant and Catholic in the Outer Hebrides that has led to bloodshed in other places, as in Holland and France in previous centuries or as in Ireland today. Perhaps this has something to do with living on small islands and knowing people as individuals. It could be however that there is rather less tolerance today, even though there is also rather less religion. If this is the case it is due to the recent changes in county boundaries. The northern half of the Outer Hebrides had previously been administered by Inverness and the southern, Catholic half by Argyll. Now however, they are one entity — The Western Isles, with the seat of administration in the Free Church stronghold of Stornoway — 'The last Bastion of Christianity' as Barra folk sarcastically refer to it. The members of the decision making council of which Catholics form only a small part are known as the 'Ayatollahs of the North'.

FOUR

The church in this island is called Kilbar, i.e., St. Barr's Church. There is a little chapel by it, in which Macneil and those descended from his family are usually interred.

Martin Martin

Every island seems to have one special place which is its true centre and from where it draws its unique and particular ethos. In Barra this spot is a rocky knoll, half-way along the slender northern peninsula of Eoligarry. It is on the same area of machair that had so enchanted the seven-year-old Elizabeth. A narrow neck joins the peninsula to the main body of the island, with a road running along its more sheltered eastern side. I seldom used this road, but took the Tank across the machair above it, so that I could keep to the crest of the low central ridge and enjoy the views of the spectacular beaches which lie on either side. The one to the west is the sandy beach of Traigh Eais, which stretches straight as an arrow for over a mile, an unbroken white margin on which the long Atlantic seas break. On the east is the Traigh Mor, a vast cockle-shell strand, which at low tide exposes a sheltered area of harder, darker sand, which holds a little surface water that reflects back the patterns of scudding clouds. It teems with life and is the noisy meeting place for flocks of raucous seabirds who flock there to feed on shellfish and lug worms.

The knoll comes just beyond the northern reach of both beaches and is where St. Finbar landed and built his cell when he came, to Christianise the island in the 6th century. He had travelled there like all the extraordinary missionary monks of that extraordinary age, crossing the rough, rock-strewn seas from Ireland, in frail leather curraghs; hugging the coasts where possible and island hopping where not — in this manner and at the same period, St. Brendan is thought to have reached the coast of America, going by way of the Faroes and Iceland. While the rest of Europe and Britain was still locked in the Dark Ages, Ireland was enjoying its Golden Age of culture and religion and was sending out 'saints' in droves to bring Christianity to every part of these remote Western Isles. Following the eremitic practices of the Eastern Church there was hardly an isolated rock at this time which didn't have a Celtic monk living out his life on it, in prayer and solitude — the remains of their cells and chapels are still visible on many of them. Where the chapels were in accessible places, as with this one on Barra, they provided a focus for ongoing worship throughout the centuries, so it is no wonder that they exude a special atmosphere, as powerful as a cathedral or any centre of prayer.

The stones of St. Finbar's original cell — Cille Bharra and those of the chapels which succeeded it have been incorporated into a burial ground, which is quite the most beautiful and cheerful of such places, most unlike the usual cemetery. It is on a gentle slope, separated from the rest of the hillside by only a low drystone wall and there are wide views over the Sound of Barra and across the Traigh Mor and the Minch, towards the blue mainland hills. The wind blows freely over it all and there is none of that hint of dankness which hangs over so many graveyards. This is in part due to the fact that the grass is kept mown and the simple headstones are set into the turf without ornate trappings or fussy paths dividing them, so that the place seems also to be pervaded by a kindly sense of equality and comradeship.

Compton Mackenzie is buried here, alongside his old friend, the piper Calum Johnston, who had insisted on piping the coffin to the graveside, despite the wild, wet weather which had prevailed on the day of the funeral. Practically as old and frail as C.M. himself, he had not survived the drenching and so the two old men lie there together, like an ancient chieftain with his faithful retainer — an incident that could have come straight from the pages of one of Compton Mackenzie's own novels and no-one who has read his books could doubt the delight it would have afforded him.

The house that Compton Mackenzie had built for himself is just a stone's throw from Cille Bharra, at the edge of the Traigh Mor, which serves as Barra's airfield. It must have been one of the lowest cost airports in the world, for nothing at all was needed to be done to the beach, to enable the planes from Glasgow to make their scheduled flights in and out, tide permitting. Even the wind sock wasn't strictly necessary as the local lady, who at the outset was the sum total of the ground staff used to talk the pilots down in a practical and concrete fashion, while she sat in the control shed, finishing off a different kind of sock.

'There's a wee bit of wind down here right enough, but nothing to worry you.' She'd radio up to them, as they circled overhead, above the cloud, 'If you bring her in over Murdo Mor's croft, you'll set her down with no bother at all.'

I gather that the pilots had the utmost trust in her assessments of the conditions and brought their aeroplanes in and out with never a disaster or even a hiccup.

I spent hours on Eoligarry, quite sharing Elizabeth's childhood enthusiasm for it, and it was there one day that I met Jim and Doris, an aged but sprightly English couple, holidaying in a camper van of small dimensions but great ingenuity. Both were very keen on prehistoric monuments, standing stones, ley lines and all matters psychical. Doris was a self-confessed white witch, firmly convinced of her presentient gifts and certain of her ability to influence events, 'in either direction' she confessed darkly. She told me several stories to illustrate her powers, Jim seriously nodding his head throughout to show his agreement and support.

Doris had first become aware of her precognitive ability at the beginning of the last war, when she was about sixteen. One day, she said, she had conceived a terrible dread of her London home; every time she closed her eyes she could see it engulfed in flames and hear terrible screams coming from it. Her mother had taken her off to Southend just to humour her and a few days later one of the first bombs of the war had obliterated the London house, landing squarely on it so that when all the rubble was cleared away there was a gap in the terrace like an extracted tooth.

Another incident had to do with a motorcyclist who had treated her son badly and whose doom she had not only predicted, but also rather wished for in the heat of the moment. He had crashed dramatically (though fortunately not quite fatally) within seconds of her maledictions, less than fifty yards away from where she was standing. Ever afterwards, she told me, with a shudder, she had kept a guard on her feelings and on her tongue, and had stuck to safer pursuits, like 'pendulum swinging' — to determine the sex of unborn babies, palm reading and an occasional 'dabble with the Tarot'.

I found Doris's stories endlessly fascinating and I enjoyed the company of them both. Their energy and enthusiasm for new experiences seemed totally undiminished by age and although their life story was nothing special, they gave the impression of having relished every bit of it, which is not all that common. Doris had never returned to the east end of London but had stayed on in Southend throughout the war years, working as a land girl and meeting Jim, a farm labourer there. After the war they had married and gone north where Jim had changed his job, becoming a miner, because the pay was so much better. One of Doris's presentiments had kept Jim out of a pit disaster, after which he felt he 'owed something' and had volunteered to serve out his time in mine rescue work. Retired now, they lived frugally, in a council house in an unattractive northern town and spent as much time as possible touring around in their camper van in the remoter parts of Britain. They had come to the Outer Hebrides several times and felt they could happily stay there forever — I never did quite decide whether this was because of the natural beauty of the islands or because of the presence of the supernatural (which Doris assured me was stronger in the Outer Hebrides than anywhere else in Britain, including Stonehenge).

Where Doris was gregarious and unendingly chatty, with masses of wild, steel-grey hair, which, she told me gleefully, enhanced her witchcraft image at home — Jim was the opposite, a quiet, gentle, unobtrusive man who seemed to be in a perpetual state of wonder at the world he found himself in. He liked best to just sit at the sea's edge, simply taking in the scene and whatever passed in front of him and he could stay there, motionless for hours. He mostly held a fishing rod loosely in his hands, not to try and catch anything, but because he thought it made people feel uncomfortable when they saw him sitting so still, doing nothing. Though if people did notice Jim's line lying along the sand in the crystal clear water where no fish could possibly be, it probably bothered them far more.

Barra being so small and having so few roads meant that one was always bumping into people one had met before and every time I came across Jim and Doris, I was invited in for coffee and a slice of Doris's delicious cake. It was in their van that I first tasted Barra cockles, a gastronomic delight that was totally unexpected, since previously I'd thought that cockles were rather nasty, small rubbery things, steeped in vinegar and served in small saucers at seafood stalls. Barra cockles, dug from the Traigh Mor at low tide were huge and succulent, something like scallops but with unique and delicate flavour. Sautéd in butter, with a dash of cayenne pepper and a squeeze of lemon, they were as good as any shellfish I have eaten. As far as I know there is no hotel on the island serving this free and delicious local food, though the shells themselves are collected in enormous quantities and made into a harling, which is sent all over Britain to coat the walls of houses. The small factory where the process is carried out is the sprawling bungalow on the edge of the Traigh Mor, which was Compton Mackenzie's former home.

Doris knew I was sceptical about her witchcraft (though out of affection for her, I would never have dreamed of saying so) nevertheless this did not deter her from trying out her healing powers on my injured foot and she would get me to sit on a chair with the leg stretched out in front of me, the heel resting on her lap, while she placed her hands around the ankle. Silent for once and visibly concentrating with eyes closed, she moved her hands up and down the plaster for several minutes, shaking her hands between strokes as though getting rid of drops of water from her fingers. I can't really say what the effect (if anything) of this was because unfortunately the situation made me want to giggle and controlling the impulse took most of my attention. But it did seem that I could feel heat from her hands passing through the thickness of the plaster and the foot certainly never hurt at all while she was holding it. Not that it was giving much pain anyway in its protective carapace, except when I'd over used it, and really it was the other foot which suffered most, as I was always scraping the plaster across the ankle bone in my sleep. However, I feel it only fair to report that the repair of the tendons which Mr. Moses had predicted would take five months was completed in three.

The single most delightful thing about Doris and Jim was the warmth of their relationship. It wasn't anything they said or did, just something that was there in every glance and gesture they directed towards each other. So it seemed strange to meet another couple who also had this same aura of being still supremely happily married, after thirty five years of that state. This was a resident couple of white settlers — Jack and Polly Huntington whom I met through a chance introduction and it was because they lived in the old Protestant manse that I was at first keen to take up the introduction. I cycled past the house most days and it had intrigued me from the moment I first saw it, so totally different was it from any other building on Barra. It was a simple, elegant three-storey structure, with a single-storey wing on either side and with delightful, lantern-fronted attic windows. Georgian I thought, though so individual in design I could have been mistaken. It had neat lawns and flower beds in front, and a walled garden at the rear which I could gain only a tantalising glimpse into from the road. It was clear that someone had lavished a great deal of love and energy on the place and indeed that is exactly what Polly and Jack Huntington had done. They had first come to the Outer Hebrides fifteen years before and thought how they would like to live there. A little later they had seen in a periodical, an advertisement for a run-down manse in Barra and had rushed up from Devon in the middle of winter to look at it. In spite of its poor state they saw its possibilities and decided immediately to try and purchase it. It was several months before they knew that they had been successful, for the practice of house buying in this part of Scotland is to put your bid into a sealed envelope, send it in and await developments. How to get the offer right, and not wildly too high or too low; or not to lose the house for the sake of an extra small amount makes it all rather a lottery.

Perhaps there were few serious bids, for there surely can't be too many people eager to take on a three-storey, damp, decaying Georgian house, cut up into a warren of small, dark, cubby holes, with a huge walled garden behind, rank with decades of neglect. When added to these disadvantages, the house is on a remote island, where whatever building work needs doing will (outside of shipping in a task force or a contractor) almost certainly be done by you or not be done at all, perhaps it doesn't seem after all, too much of a miracle that Jack and Polly got their manse.

What they have done with the place however does seem a little miraculous and the thought 'House and Garden' comes inevitably to mind because the first impression is of an overall, quiet elegance. Nothing could really be further from that glossy, flawless image however, as Polly is a true original and has the sort of innate taste and unfaltering touch that can make something lovely of a handful of stones thrown down at random, or an old linen sheet pulled over a wire to serve as a cupboard door. A lot of the decorations have been gathered off the beaches and every deep window ledge has its collection of shells, corals, bleached and twisted branches and a host of the other infinitely varied wonders, tossed up by the sea. Much of the furnishings — beds, chairs, mirrors, tables etc. came from the island rubbish tip, where they had been discarded in favour of mass-produced goods from mail-order catalogues, and were rescued and lovingly restored by Polly. Mixed in with their few good paintings, fine porcelain and the furniture which came from more conventional sources, the result is an interior full of unusual charm and interest.

Jack, a lawyer by training but hardly by practice, has followed many pursuits, including that of a London art dealer, but houses and particularly gardens seem to have been a more enduring passion, which a small private income, lots of energy and a growing skill at D.I.Y. has enabled him to indulge to a point where it was difficult to fit in gainful employment. However, funds were so tight when they first arrived, he took on the job of third assistant-lighthouse-keeper on Barra Head, the southerly tip of the Outer Hebrides (the lighthouse has since been made fully automatic). The helicopter which whisked him off for his spells of duty used to land on the lawn at the front of the manse and Jack said it always amazed him each time that he actually was given wages for a job that was such a delight. Apparently he got the position purely on the strength of his culinary skills. The interview had been conducted with the lighthouse keeper yelling down to Jack, who was as near to the lighthouse as a boat could bring him, pitching about in the uneasy waters.

'Can ye cook?' the keeper had bellowed down and Jack's 'like an angel' had clinched the matter. Jack said that after he had sampled the preparations of the other two keepers, he had understood the burning importance of the question and in the interest of survival had taken over all the cooking on his tours of duty.

Between spells in the lighthouse, he and Polly had worked on the house, tearing down the extraneous partitions and laying bare the lovely proportions of the original rooms, which went from back to front of the house with light coming in from windows on either side. Plumbing, slating, cementing, whatever needed doing, they did themselves and when the house was more or less weather-tight, they turned their attentions to the grounds and to transforming the rampaging wilderness outside.

To complement the facade of the house they had planted trees, shrubs, flowers and lawns and generally landscaped the land at the front, but most of their efforts have been concentrated in the walled garden at the rear. They now grow a wealth of fine sturdy vegetables of great variety, which they and an unending stream of visitors eat all the year round, and still have a surplus to sell. What a difference fresh vegetables make to island life is not difficult for a traveller to appreciate, after making do for weeks with tinned or frozen vegetables or with the limp and decaying 'fresh' ones which, like poor wines, just don't travel well. I was tremendously impressed by this burgeoning market garden.

The salt-laden wind is the main enemy of gardeners on coasts exposed to Atlantic gales, so Jack and Polly divided up the garden with slatted wood fencing to provide additional shelter, combing the beaches for the wood, and then they dug and dug the whole thing, over and over, by hand, for the ground has too many concealed boulders in it to use a rotovator. Polly's skills are apparent everywhere in the garden too, even among the vegetables where islands of the discarded rocks, planted about with herbs, or flowers make contrasts of texture and form. It has finished up looking as though it owed as much to the ideas of Japanese formal gardens, as to a conventional market garden. The almost completed task seems a tremendous achievement for two people, especially considering that Jack and Polly were middle-aged when they began the project and had already reared and launched their family of four daughters.

It was the vegetables that brought home to me the essential difference between the indigenous islanders and the white settlers. Very few Barra folk other than the serious full time farmers now grow anything, not even the potatoes which are an essential item of their diet. Elizabeth found this the single most striking change in life style when she returned home after leaving the island to begin her teaching career. She told me that it was the greenness of the untilled ground that first struck them when they returned, especially after the war.

'When I was a girl, every scrap of land was turned for the spring planting, so the ground was black and the sheep were away up in the hills with the other beasts. There weren't so many sheep then of course and a good thing too — the nuisance that they are now with all their mess. Every house would grow their own potatoes and turnips too and some would grow carrots and cabbages and I mind others that came back with swanky notions and grew all manner of strange things none of the rest would touch. But it got that fewer and fewer would put spade to ground.'

Many and ingenious are the reasons offered by the islanders for leaving their land untended year after year and their fences broken so that the ubiquitous sheep feel free to wander all over the crofts and scratch themselves against the cottage walls.

'Ach you can't grow that here,' is said of every single vegetable you care to mention and if you press for a reason, its — 'Ach the soil's no good for it.' 'The weeds will swamp it just' or 'We don't get the growing weather anymore, the summers are terrible.'

But the truth is that few can be bothered anymore. An alien set of values has totally eroded their former way of life, before the people concerned were in any position to know what was happening, or to exercise any choice in relation to the change. It is easier for incomers to opt for the simple life style and turn their back on accepted norms and standards. They know what they are giving up and are able to choose what they see as an enhanced quality of life in place of greater material rewards. People trapped in poverty, or with a much tighter and interdependent social structure are not in a position to make such choices and the effect on them of the onslaught of a more materialistic culture is devastating and nearly always destructive to their traditional values. This can be seen all over the Third World today as countries like Nepal struggle to become westernised overnight, destroying in the process the very things that Western man is beginning to find lacking in his own society. The same process has already happened in the Outer Hebrides and it is quite understandable that the casual visitor observing all the weed-covered, unworked land is puzzled about what the economy can possibly be. The culture I had been at such pains to discover before it disappeared altogether was already just a memory in Barra.

I stayed for a few days with an island family who were farming an area of land which had once been several crofts. They grew hay and cereals for the winter feeding of their sheep and nothing else at all except for a few potatoes. They didn't even keep hens, and they fed themselves, their three children and an aged mother who lived with them, mostly on convenience foods shipped over from the mainland. They had two television sets in their small house, both of which stayed on from first light to the end of the last programme. Everyone watched the screen all the time, even during meals, or when they were talking to someone and when I was alone one day with the wife, Morag, she told me (still with half her attention on the television) of how she was so desperately unhappy, that it was only with the utmost difficulty that she could face each day. She had no idea why she felt like this. On the face of it 'they had never been so well off' an E.E.C. grant had renovated and improved the croft house out of all recognition. Subsidies and further grants ensured a standard of living never enjoyed before. True it was trying having her invalid mother there and her husband had only recently been cured of chronic alcoholism, but none of that could really account for the despair she was feeling. If she didn't tell someone she thought she'd go mad.

Listening to Morag's sad unburdening, I felt I could have been hearing the story of a lonely isolated woman in a derelict inner-city area, and yet here I was in one of the most beautiful places (albeit also the wettest) in Britain, which had a living tradition of strong social support. But I was also aware of the very high rate of suicide, alcoholism and drug taking in these parts, for there have been many studies on the subject in the last few years. Some make a correlation between depression and northern latitudes, claiming that the further north, the greater the level of depression and the larger the quantity of alcohol consumed, especially by the men. Others blame culture shock and see the break up of communities and the erosion of traditional life styles as leading to an isolation more profound than that existing in the inner cities. Morag certainly seemed isolated in a way that was remarkable, considering she lived on such a small island where she knew a good proportion of the population.

It is from the land itself that the greatest alienation seems to be, and I first became aware of this as I got to know Morag's children. They were like most lively youngsters, eager to learn about the natural things around them and yet strangely they hardly ever roamed about and they knew practically nothing of their island, not even the names (Gaelic or English) of the wild flowers, birds, animals or sea creatures. The sort of knowledge about the surrounding countryside which is normally handed down from parents to children, had entirely passed them by. It wasn't that they preferred playing on bicycles or watching television, for they were always eager to accompany me, and when I took them down to the shore, they spent hours peering fascinated into rock pools and asked endless questions about what they saw. Other island children also showed this same lack of intimacy with their surroundings and I came to the conclusion that going for walks and generally becoming acquainted with their natural heritage was something today's children were likely to do only if they had a teacher keen on nature study.

I began to realise that there was really nothing at all to take many Barra folk out of their houses any longer, except the need to collect pensions, do the shopping and attend church, and a car, or pensioners' bus is mostly used for these errands. No-one even cuts peat in Barra now, one activity which still leads people to spend many hours in the open air in other islands. Hardly anyone keeps a cow on the common grazing, or has really anything at all which makes them a country as opposed to an urban people. With no necessity to venture forth in the so often inclement weather, people lose the close contact with the land that comes from the daily familiarity and the unending struggle between man and nature which shaped the preceding generations.

Faced with the problems of the Outer Hebrides, especially with unemployment, as high as anywhere in Britain, it is difficult not to feel nostalgic about a way of life all but vanished, which though unrelentingly hard, also seemed to have offered so much in the way of social and spiritual fulfilment. Successive governments have tried various remedies to reverse the decline of the crofting communities (too little, too late it is normally thought) but with no real success, for one essential fact remains — few people today value a way of life that is so unendingly demanding and at the same time so sparse in material rewards. The ambitious and most successful youngsters continue to leave, seeking a better future elsewhere, while the average age of the remaining community continues to rise.

As involvement in the land decays, so attention is increasingly focused on material comforts, housing in particular. A fever of modernisation and improvement, in the Dallas 'ranchitis' style has swept the kitchens of Barra in a sea of simulated wood formica and gadgetry. The quasi-Georgian town-house door (the D.I.Y. success story of the decade) is now the incongruous entrance of many traditional island cottages. The latest fashions in clothes and hairstyles arrive only weeks behind the Metropolis and the same expensive BMX bicycles lie in rusting piles outside the school. As with the cloned shopping precincts of the average British town, it is as though the islands are attempting to become indistinguishable from anywhere else.

With so few people concerned with the immediate world outside their doors, it is of real concern as to how long these Western Isles will remain as unravished and available as they are at present. Fifty miles out to sea is magnificent St. Kilda with the highest, most spectacular sea cliffs in Britain, the remnant of its unique culture was evacuated fifty years ago and it is now just a platform for sophisticated rocket-tracking equipment.

There are islands which have already been used for even darker purposes, like Gruinard, which was deliberately infected with anthrax in 1941, in an official government experiment that rendered it highly and horribly toxic for years to come — and it has only just, in 1988, been declared safe after an astronomical expenditure. There are notions of using the area to dump nuclear waste, and pressures for establishing N.A.T.O. bases, not to mention the environmentally destructive potential of present oil exploration plans.

FIVE

The steward of the Lesser and Southern Islands is reckoned a great man here, in regard of the perquisites due to him; such as a particular share of all the lands, corn, butter, cheese, fish etc. which these islands produce.

Martin Martin

To THE SOUTH OF BARRA, ARE NINE small islands which form the tail of the Outer Hebrides, some of them are little more than large sea-girt rocks, but each 'had ane chapell in everie ile perteining to the Bischop of the Isles' wrote Dean Munro in 1549. This indefatigable churchman was the first person known to have compiled a list of Hebridean islands — about 250 of them — from personal observation. He was more fortunate than I in being able to visit every one of Barra's southern neighbours and to find them all 'inhabite and manurit' and most of them 'verie gude for corn and fishing'.

Only Vatersay, the largest of these islands and the closest to Barra has any inhabitants left today, other than sheep and seabirds, and even Vatersay's days are numbered, local people say, unless a causeway or a bridge is built soon. From around the back of the hill on Barra, where I damaged my foot, it is barely a couple of hundred yards to Vatersay's most northerly point, but it would mean constructing more than a mile of road to gain access to this narrow point, as well as the cost of the bridge itself, and that for a population of less than a hundred. Vatersay is reached at present by ferry from Castlebay with a good mile of water to cross and that has made the business of courtship difficult for the island males. The plight of these 'Bachelors of Vatersay' made national headlines a short while ago and there was even talk of appealing to the European Court of

Human Rights, but finally there is a scheme for a bridge in hand.

The people of Vatersay have a tradition for being prepared to go all out for their rights. During the 19th Century every one of the original families had been evicted to Barra's rocky east coast and the whole island was turned into one private farm. In the agitation for more ground by the desperately overcrowded and land-hungry people of Barra, following the Crofting Act of 1886, the descendants of those original Vatersay folk tried to get back their old crofts by the simple expedient of moving in and building houses on them; their spokesman informing the Secretary of State that —

'Their grandparents and remoter ancestors had crofts on Vatersay at the very place where the raiders' huts are now set up — and though their grandparents had been evicted their descendants had never given up their claim. Throughout all the years their descendants down to this day have continued to bury their dead on Vatersay.'

Prison sentences were meted out to the 'raiders' but undeterred they returned after each sentence, until eventually the proprietor, Lady Gordon Cathcart, was persuaded to sell the island to the Congested Districts Board. She held out until her ridiculously inflated price of £6,250 was met, after which the raiders were all granted permanent holdings.

I had taken Evans the Tank across with me to explore Vatersay, for the map showed four miles of road and track, as well as machair to ride on and as yet I could walk only for a few hundred yards with my crutches. It was a lovely island to explore by bicycle and my eighteen low gears made light work of the steepest places there. My first impression was much the same as Dean Munro had found 'ane faire mayne Ile'. But the trouble with 'faire' for describing these islands is that every one of them is fair and there are just not enough adjectives to describe all the different kinds and degrees of 'faireness', nor are there words to convey the infinite subtle variety, that makes each island such a unique and different place. But 'faire' I most certainly found Vatersay, in some ways the loveliest of them all with so much gentle, fertile grassland and such an extended coastline of curved white beaches. On many of these beaches lay the wooden skeletons of wrecked ships and abandoned boats — black ribs against the bright sky, so much more poignant than decaying cars. Along with the dead boats were also many dead weed-choked crofts with their abandoned houses, each with its blind windows looking out over views of unparalleled magnificence. It was hard to accept that the descendants of those raiders, who just seventy years ago had fought with such tenacity to reclaim these acres should voluntarily relinquish their rights to them.

Over the millennia, the sea has gnawed away at Vatersay until it has become almost two islands, joined together by a narrow belt of sand-edged machair. The main settlement and the ancient burial site is south of this natural causeway in a sheltered hollow with a small fresh-water loch. It has the feel of being the true centre of the island from time immemorial. Because of this I found it even harder to forgive the terrible new council housing which had replaced the earlier cottages. It wasn't so much the design of the individual units that was objectionable, they were quite a pleasant Scandinavian type that looked as though they could be quite snug and convenient to live in — except that is for the fact that they are 'all electric' and Vatersay people still cut peats for their fuel, or rather the rest of the islanders still do. There wouldn't be much point in the council house people cutting peats any more since their new houses don't have fireplaces to burn them in. The electricity comes from Uist by underwater cable to Barra and then by another underwater cable to Vatersay — a vulnerable route for the sole power supply. The worst aspect of the development however and the one that confirms that it was designed without any consideration for the locality in which it was to be built is that all the houses are squashed together into a square block, with a tiny communal space at the rear as though they were part of an estate in a crowded inner city, or a defensive structure in hostile territory. Space is the one commodity which is not in short supply in these islands now. The old cottages still stand around the perimeter of what had once been the casual Hebridean version of a village green. Each one in sight of the others, but each occupying its own space with an air of individuality and independence. No doubt it makes economic sense in terms of drains and other services, to build houses cheek by jowl, but what is the point of living somewhere as remote as the Outer Hebrides and not being able to raise your voice without the neighbours hearing? That seems to be merely taking on urban pressures and disadvantages without any of the advantages.

I had intended to visit several more of the Bishops Isles, Pabbay, Berneray and Mingulay in particular. There was a consortium of Barra crofters who had the grazing rights to them and kept sheep there and I was to go out with these men to photograph the annual shearing. The unsettled weather made planning these trips very difficult however, for it is not a good idea to shear the fleeces when they're wet and the two fine days in a row which are necessary seemed only to happen at weekends when we couldn't go because of Sunday. Though why this should be so was something I never quite understood, as Barra folk were on the whole very relaxed about the Sabbath. At mass in Castlebay, people were heading for the door before the priest had reached the vestry and while the last hymn was still being sung. It seemed a somewhat uninhibited ending to a church service, but I was told it was the only sensible procedure as everyone was bound for the shops which opened immediately after mass and there would be a terrible crush if they all arrived together.

The one occasion the weather was right and the shearers got to Mingulay, I was away in Uist at the hospital. So I waited on in the hope of eventually being able to photograph the shearing on Pabbay, which was also reputed to have some ancient carved stones which I was keen to see.

In the meantime I discovered another way of getting to Mingulay, which was with a local motor boat whose owner was prepared to make the round trip if enough people had assembled on the pier and if he himself wasn't suffering a hangover. I happened to be around on a rare sunny day one day when both these conditions proved favourable and without hesitation I abandoned Evans and hobbled aboard. The boy who was helping the passengers step down from the quay eyed my lameness dubiously and asked me if I knew I had to jump ashore at Mingulay? Well yes, I did know and I also knew that I'd already been mistreating my foot shamefully. The plaster had been removed a few days before and now it was merely strapped up and had a nasty tendency to turn over at the slightest provocation; I was still supposed to use crutches and take only moderate exercise. However, once the island bug has bitten someone, even if that person is normally sensible, he (or she) can no longer really be trusted to behave rationally when occasions arise to indulge their obsession, and this was the case with me. I felt I had to seize this opportunity to visit Mingulay and hang the consequences. I left my crutches with Evans and told the boy that I was suffering from nothing worse than a little stiffness.

The voyage out was the closest I was to get to Sandray, Pabbay and Muldonich, mere glimpses as we slid past, just enough to whet the appetite for future trips. Berneray, the southernmost island, we had not expected to see at all, but did so because two lighthouse technicians had to be put ashore there to do a few hours maintenance on the automatic light. Apart from Berneray which has a pier and a road across to the lighthouse, the other islands seemed to have reverted completely to nature and I found it difficult to imagine them as the corn-bearing, fertile isles the Dean described.

Writing a hundred and fifty years after Dean Munro, a young factor from Skye, Martin Martin, also described the islands as very fertile. Berneray, just 'two miles in circumference', he claimed, 'excells all other islands of the same extent for cultivation and fishing.' He added that 'the natives never go fishing while Macneil or his steward is around, lest seeing their plenty of fish, perhaps they might take occasion to raise the rent.'

Martin Martin's description of the islands is valuable particularly for the details of husbandry and social practices he gives, which are absent in Dean Munro's much shorter account. Martin made his study at a turning point in history when the old order was about to be swept away. Dr. Johnson who read the book was thought to have been inspired by it to make his own Hebridean journey in 1773 (during which he continually bemoaned the fact that he was already too late to observe the vanished life-style). Martin portrays the not unenviable way of life of a paternalistic society, where tenants and chief acknowledge their mutual dependency, as for example when someone's partner dies.

'When a tenant's wife in the adjacent island dies, he then addresses himself to Macneil of Barra representing his loss, and at the same time desires that he would be pleased to recommend a wife to him, without which he cannot manage his affairs, nor beget followers to Macneil, which would prove a public loss to him. Upon this representation, Macneil finds out a suitable match for him; and the woman's name being told to him, he goes to her, carrying a bottle of strong water for their entertainment at the marriage, which is then consummated.'

A tenant's widow was entitled to demand the same match-making service, according to Martin, who further outlines the duties of the chief 'if a milk-cow was lost through misfortune, Macneil made good the loss and in all things made certain that the tenants did not "want for necessities of sustenance".' Most impressive of all is his statement that old men, no longer capable of work were taken into Macneil's own family to be cared for until death.

Several other passengers had also been speculating on the vanished cultures of these islands and as they too had been reading up their Dean Munro and Martin Martin, there was a good deal of discussion and pooling of information. One man in particular was extremely knowledgeable and firmly put the rest of us right when we had erroneously equated this paternalistic clan system with the Welfare State.

'What you must realise,' he said, 'was that in the clan system, every one had a real value and responsibility. The tenant and the chief knew that neither could exist without the other, so although the chief had an almost exhalted position, there was an essential if strange equality too. They were members of one family and the tenant asking the chief to find him a wife was not servilely seeking permission to marry but reminding his chief of his duty to provide a necessity of life for him; at the same time he was tacitly confirming his unswerving loyalty to the chief's service. I don't think that people can possibly feel that sort of loyalty towards something as remote and impersonal as the Welfare State.' Warming to his subject, he continued: 'It was more than a total economic packet, it provided food, family, work, law, entertainment, morality, and a single belief system, and since the chief couldn't exert authority without the tacit support of his tenantry, it could also be said that it was a true democracy. No wonder the English were determined to smash clan loyalty after Culloden; it was a powerful force.'

That was as far as he was allowed to get since many people were eager to challenge several points he had made, particularly the one about democracy, but it all had to be left in the air anyway as the boat had drawn up against the eastern rocks of Mingulay and we had to hurry to leap ashore and climb up into the island while the tide was right. After that we all scattered like the sheep into the interior and did not see each other again until we assembled for the homeward journey several hours later, when everyone was too tired and replete with island scenery to wish to continue the discussion.

Mingulay is a giant sun trap — one central fertile valley lying between two sheltering hills, and tilting down to the east from the western cliffs, which are second in height and grandeur only to those on St. Kilda — sheer, black slabs with the precarious nests of kittiwakes miraculously clinging to barely perceptible ledges and fulmars playing on the up-draughts of the wind. I would have been unrepentant about my decision to make the trip to Mingulay for those cliffs alone I thought, as I turned my back reluctantly upon them and hobbled painfully down the lovely bowl-like valley to where the boat would be picking us up. Through the centre of the valley wound a brook of clear, good water, falling through a succession of small pools fringed with water plants, in which I bathed my ankle at the frequent stops I made. On the sides of the southern hill, Hecla, were the remains of stone dykes marking out the former fields, the patterns of furrows still showing plainly in the green turf. The slopes of Macphees Hill to the north and the rest of the island was uncultivated pasturage. All over the close-cropped turf of the valley floor was the evidence of an extensive rabbit population. They had all descended from a single pair, introduced by shepherds after the evacuation of the island — meat for the pot during the shearing season. At the eastern end of the glen a creamy-coloured beach sheltered the roofless remains of the village, half buried in the sand, with a green track leading to an upper portion over a shoulder of Hecla. Raised up on a low knoll to the left was a two-storied building with an outside staircase to the top floor and a large hole in the slated roof and other signs of galloping decay. This had been the priest's house with the upper floor serving as a chapel and as is often the way with these things, it had not been built long before the island was abandoned.

The absence of a good harbour was the main cause of the demise of Mingulay (ironically this, together with the remoteness had also preserved her from rapacious 18th and 19th century land grabbers). Cut off, sometimes for months at a time, life on Mingulay was one of considerable isolation. In the rapidly changing social climate of the 20th century people began to find such isolation no longer bearable and in 1908, the menfolk of Mingulay had joined the other raiders on Vatersay.

My foot having got me as far as the priest's house refused to have anything further to do with exploration, so I was unable to take a closer look at the old village houses and for the remaining hour before the boat returned to take us off, I thought I had better rest by the wall of what had been the garden of the manse. It was clear that this building must have been occupied for quite a considerable period after the evacuation. Closer to I realised that it was still in use, despite the dilapidation. Having been the holiday home of various people and a temporary shelter for sheep and their shearers from time to time, it is now the property of a young man called Colin who had just been spending a couple of weeks there and was about to depart on the boat after closing up the house — as far as you can secure a property with an outsize hole in the roof which has extended to a large hole in the floor beneath it.

Colin kindly let me sit there and wash up various things for him, while he made us both coffee and told me all about the place. He had bought it a year or two before, for the simple reason that he didn't think it should be allowed to fall down. It had become his mission and so strong was his devotion to the place, that I think he had become blind to most of its faults and in his eyes it was only a little short of perfect. He had a job, teaching in Germany and being unmarried was able to plough every penny he earned into this large, remotely-situated, white elephant. The previous year he had left money for some workmen on Barra to get the place watertight. They had found mending the roof either too difficult or too draughty for them and had instead spent their time lining the inside walls with plaster board. This of course had not been improved by the rain which could still come in quite freely.

I couldn't help feeling that Colin's missionary zeal might have been better employed on some more worthwhile project, though I admired him deeply for his single mindedness and certainly shared his enthusiasm for Mingulay. The house itself though was too far gone structurally to be saved by the odd bit of cobbling here and there. Lintels had slipped, large cracks had opened up in the thick masonry — you could almost hear it coming apart, groaning in travail; nor was it possible to miss the smell of decay and dampness attacking from every side, as well as from above and below. Even on this sunny day it made me shudder rather to be inside it. My abiding memory of the interior is of the mammoth collection of empty whisky bottles adorning the mantelshelves, in rows three deep. Their presence could perhaps help to explain how a perfectly sane young man was able to sustain so impossible a dream. We finished the last bottle outside in the sunshine, before the boat came, which helped considerably in getting my over-worked ankle down the rocks.

That was the last of the sun for several days. During the night clouds started edging in, blotting out the stars and before morning I was securing the storm door of the tent, as rain came lashing down on a north-easterly wind. Thanks to this weather I became involved with another island interior, one belonging to Thetis whom I first met on the MacBrayne ferry and again when we had both been dining with Polly and Jack Huntington. On both occasions she had invited me to call and when finally I did, I was so wet that I arrived on her doorstep feeling as though I had swum there. I had packed up the tent as there was now so much water in the burn I had to cross, that I had decided to move from the loch-side camp. Fairly damp already from ferrying all the gear across, I had gone to have lunch in the comfort of the bar in Northbay and had sat on long past closing time, watching Wimbledon and hoping that the rain might at least ease off. It had not done so and when I finally thought I'd better go before I should be shamed by being thrown out, I found that some-one had stolen my cycling cape − a quite extraordinary happening for a part of Britain where one can safely leave anything lying about anywhere for months. I think it must have been taken by an ill-equipped visitor who was unable to resist the temptation of a water-proof garment in such inclement conditions. Without it I was soaked to the skin in no time and I think it was a great act of charity on Thetis's part, not to express any sign of horror at having this drowned rat of a visitor, creating pools of water all over her kitchen floor.

I had intended moving in to a B&B for the remainder of my stay on Barra but Thetis wouldn't hear of it, she had a spare room upstairs 'crying out to be made use of' and she would be only too glad of a little company in the bleak weather. There was even room for poor rain-battered Evans, who was beginning to show bright orange streaks of rust and was more in need of a roof over his head than I was. The chance to work on him under cover and the pres-ence of a much needed oilcan convinced me I was in the right place and I accepted the kind offer, and so added Thetis to the list of friends I made on Barra.

Thetis had lived a free and adventurous life, travelling extensively in the Middle East, where a famous exploring ancestor had made his name and where, doubtless, even earlier ancestors had fought in the Crusades and come back with a taste for the refinements and luxur-ies of the Arab world. Certainly Thetis's family had continued to flourish, albeit fairly modestly, having remained Roman Catholic, which was seldom an easy or a profitable thing to be in Britain, after Henry VIII. With the death of her only brother in the First World War, the line had come to an abrupt end. At some time, Thetis had found time to marry and had raised a daughter, but now she was on her own, an old-age pensioner, in fairly straightened circumstances and often quite lonely I think.

Thetis really loved Barra and has managed to remain on the island in spite of the difficulty of finding suitable accommodation. She sur-vived for over a year in a caravan − never a relaxed existence espe-cially in the season of Atlantic gales, when even vans well-lashed down, have been blown into the sea. Earlier in the year, through the good offices of her friends, she had found this small cottage to rent. It was in one of the once overcrowded townships on the east coast, which I tended to think, still wore a depressed air, though this could be due to the fact that I always saw it in the rain, with wet sheep huddling for shelter around the few bedraggled bushes and the broken fences.

Inside the cottage Thetis was still in the throes of creating order, which, as it so often does, meant first creating more chaos. In particular, she was engaged in the horrid business of removing layers of old paint from the wood panelling, in what would be her sitting room. I dislike decorating, having done far too much of it over the years. Sanding down woodwork I dislike particularly, but I alternated it with removing the rust from Evans and getting him back into good working order and there was Thetis's company too which was a great delight. We talked endlessly, especially after supper when plenty of wine had damped down all the wood dust we'd swallowed — the wine was dispensed from one of those large convenient boxes with a spigot, which like all the other conveniences of modern living, have speedily made their appearance on Barra. We had many interests in common, especially the eastern lands we had both travelled in, but somehow we always got on to topics like the problems of pain, forgiveness, evil etc. Thetis was under strict spiritual direction which meant that she meditated regularly, twice a day and thought a great deal about such subjects and so was more able than I in discussing them.

Each day I phoned to see what the likelihood was of getting to Pabbay and each day I was told that the forecast looked better for the following day — the Hebridean has to be an optimist where the weather is concerned, he'd give up otherwise. I too am an optimist, but after three days of being incarcerated, even with such interesting company, I felt I had had enough and on the fourth day, I gave up, suddenly full of impatience to continue the journey. I realised that I would have to leave the remaining Bishops Isles for another year and move on northwards, in case winter found me still on Barra, waiting for a break in the weather.

Before I left I accompanied Thetis on the O.A.P.'s weekly shopping bus to Castlebay and stocked up on camp stores, remembering especially to top up the whisky flask, without which I consider it suicidal to attempt to camp in this area, and after Barra such necessities become harder to find. When I finally cycled away from the cottage after lunch, it wasn't actually raining, but the clouds were so low and thick, that a layer of moisture covered everything and everyone. My 'waterproof' jacket and trousers could keep most of this out, but without the cape, I should be soaked again if it came on to rain seriously. I bade a fond farewell to Thetis who was hoping that I'd change my mind — I was she claimed, the best wood sander to have worked on her parlour walls.

On the way to the ferry I stopped to say goodbye to Elizabeth and found that she had left the bedding ready in the priest's room, in case I'd needed to sleep on the sofa again in the awful weather — and somehow that one small incident made me realise how very fond I had become of this island and particularly of all the people who had been so open and friendly to me. Instead of being eager to depart I felt suddenly rather sad and nostalgic as though I had already abandoned something rather precious that I wasn't really able to appreciate. In this mood I cycled along Eoligarry to the ferry, while a few watery beams of sunlight shone down through ragged breaks in the dense clouds, and a flat two-dimensional rainbow spanned the road ahead.

On the machair by the jetty were Jim and Doris beckoning from their van for me to come over and have a cup of coffee with them. When they heard I was leaving on the ferry Doris lit the stove and fried up a pan of fresh Barra cockles, that Jim had dug from the sand that morning.

'You've time to eat them before the boat comes,' she said when I protested that I'd already had lunch. 'Besides there's a story that people tell round here, they say if you eat enough cockles from the Traigh Mor you'll be sure to come back to Barra before too long and you really like it here don't you?'

I don't think it needed a white witch to find that out.

CHAPTER

S I X

The island Erisca, about a mile in length and three in circumference, is partly heathy and partly arable and yields a good produce.

Martin Martin

T HERE WAS ONE PARTICULAR ISLAND in the Outer Hebrides for which I had always cherished highly romantic notions, ever since I had been taught to sing the haunting Eriskay Love Lilt as a child at school. The fact that Eriskay was also the very first place in Scotland on which 'Bonnie Prince Charlie' had set foot at the start of his ill-advised, ill-fated, but nonetheless, stirring adventure to restore the Jacobite fortunes, had done nothing to lessen my expectations of an island, somehow uniquely special. The cynicism of youth, which delights in debunking childhood fancies had had no success at all with Eriskay. In fact my expectations of it had been heightened by reading *Whisky Galore* and further raised by other claims to the island's uniqueness — it was for instance, said to have a flower that grew nowhere else in Scotland, which had sprung from seeds fallen out of the Prince's pocket; it was also claimed to have its own distinct breed of ponies; and even a design of sweater knitted there and nowhere else.

In spite of all these attractions, I hadn't yet visited Eriskay, probably because I didn't want to subject my cherished ideas about it to the cold light of reality; I feared disappointment, though I doubt I would have admitted that as the reason. Every time I'd seen the island's distinctive outline as the ferry passed by to the west of it, I'd thought this time I'll go, but when we'd reached Ludag pier, either the Eriskay boat wasn't due to leave yet or the weather had looked unpromising and I'd changed my mind and cycled north.

It lies between Barra and South Uist and has an appendage of steep, jagged rocks off its southern point, like a dragon's tail. On the last of these are the remains of what must be the ultimate in island strongholds, a small, inaccessible fort, of unknown antiquity called the Weavers Castle. The island is about two miles long and a mile wide, rising up steeply to the central peak of Ben Scrien at around 600 feet. It appears unusually well populated for its size, with houses clustered fairly close together on the west-facing slopes. Many people from South Uist were crowded on to Eriskay in the 'clearances' of the last century and without the fishing, which is still the mainstay of the island economy, they would not have survived. There is only a narrow coastal strip of arable land in the northwest corner, certainly not enough to supply the basic needs of more than a few families.

I had no real intention of going to Eriskay this time either, it was the weather that decided otherwise. Half way across the Sound of Barra, as the ferry left the shelter of the rocky headland of Fuday the wind began to blow strongly from the west and the boat started to plunge and take solid water over the foredeck where poor Evans was secured to the rails, getting rusty again. All the way across, the wind increased and rain lashed down on the broken jumble of waves driven before the wind, over the shallow banks.

Just getting off the boat and on to South Uist, at Ludag pier was an exercise in precision and I was thankful for strong island men who could swing a mountain bicycle one-handed off a pitching deck, with no trouble at all. My one thought was shelter for the night, for it was no weather to be camping. On the pier there was a bus converted into a café, a new amenity since my last visit to South Uist (I didn't count the recent journeys to the hospital as I'd been able to see very little through the darkened windows of the ambulance). Any sort of café here indicated either an increased tourist trade or a high degree of optimism. This one didn't look over-used, though it was most attractive, with fresh white paintwork, blue check-clothed tables, a small counter bearing plates of scones and a shiny tea urn, and a little girl lying fast asleep, stretched out on two hard chairs.

The mother of the child (who woke up to greet the only customer of the day) said the nearest place to stay was at a B&B on Eriskay and her husband who ran the ferry would be going over shortly when she closed the café. I asked about the bus as she dispensed tea. She had only had it for this season, she said and she was quite pleased with how it was going, at least on good days, though of course there hadn't been many of those yet this summer, had there? It had been her husband's idea to put the bus here and do it up, he was a Lewis man, the only Protestant on Catholic Eriskay and she supposed someone new to the place could always see a need where those living with it under their noses would miss it. He thought people waiting for both the ferry to Barra and to Eriskay would be glad of somewhere to sit out of the wind, where they could get a cup of tea and a bite to eat. She herself enjoyed running it; it got her off the island and gave her a bit of a change.

Having 'phoned and checked that there was a room for me, I boarded the ferry and in quarter of an hour I was on Eriskay. It certainly wasn't the arrival I'd imagined. There could be little temptation to look around in the continuing heavy downpour and all that I saw as I followed the ferryman's directions from the new, business-like pier to the B&B was a roughly-surfaced road flanked by clusters of rain-streaked houses, with a number of beat-up old cars in varying stages of sagging decrepitude crouching beside them on patches of rough, bare ground. Here and there were the crumbling remains of thick, dry-stone walls that had once enclosed tiny areas of cultivation but which now sheltered nothing more than rusting oildrums and discarded engines and such like. There was an air of dereliction that reminded me strongly of one of the more isolated bleak, coal-mining villages of the Rhondda Valley, to which I had gone as a small, reluctant evacuee in the last war. Ironically, it was in that sour, despoiled bit of Welsh landscape that I had began to form my early ideas of this Hebridean island — I would never have imagined then, that one day I would be finding similarities between the two.

A few minutes riding along an unmade track brought me, once more soaked and dripping to my night's lodging and whatever sort of accommodation I had imagined I should find on this storm-wracked shore, it was certainly not this. From the Georgian fan-lighted front door and the labour-saving, space-age kitchen, to the minute but luxuriously fitted bedrooms, it was like wandering through scenes displayed in glossy brochures, except that the small rooms were bursting at the seams with all the expensive joinery. Between my candlewick-covered twin bed with 'integral, plastic-padded, shelved, drawered and concealedly lit' (and not strong enough to read by) headboard' was a few inches of aggressive, toe-snaring, shag-piled carpet before I ran up against the 'solid mahogany louvred' doors of the built-in wardrobes. It was all rather overwhelming as though I had passed suddenly through a 'time warp'. . . and as for the bathroom, with sunken bath of unusual shape and colour, closely flanked by matching bidet, pedestal basin and so forth, that was just saved from being totally intimidating by the incongruous presence of a plastic doll dressed in a crinoline and perched on top of the low-level suite, where her crocheted skirts decorously hid the spare toilet roll.

My hostess was an incomer, from the Scottish mainland, a young woman with two small children, aged three and five. She was also the district nurse and I had not been there five minutes before she was summoned to attend someone who was having a fit. The children were obviously used to these emergencies and in no-time were out of their night clothes (they had been getting ready for bed when I arrived) and into outdoor things and away with their mother in the car. I was left to answer the telephone if it rang, which indeed it did and it turned out to be the husband of my hostess who wished to know if he was to come home or meet his wife at friends with whom they were going to spend the evening. As I couldn't answer this he came home and I had the opportunity to meet the person who had planned and carried out all the improvements on the house. He too was not island born, but had been raised on Eriskay by foster parents and had inherited the croft from them. He worked on the oil rigs and during his long spells ashore, his considerable energy was concentrated on transforming this small island house into a suburban dream. He had done almost all the work himself and however one related to the result, it was impossible not to admire the skill and sustained effort that had gone into it. Now it was all but finished, I wondered what he would find to fill in his hours of leisure.

They were a friendly, hospitable couple and when they saw that I was interested in the islands, they arranged for an old Eriskay man to come over for a chat with me, while they were out. This was Donald MacKinnis, known as Dold Beag (Little Donald) to distinguish him from his father, long since dead. He was a gentle, very thin old man, with silver hair and a very dark suntanned skin, who had served a lifetime in the merchant navy. He couldn't have been much less than eighty but looked more like sixty. He came in to sit with me in the kitchen walking with some trepidation across the shiny vinyl floor, as though he feared to leave mud on it. Across the hall, the young island girl who was baby sitting gave up the struggle to keep the five year old girl in bed and together they sat in the lounge, watching endless television programmes, all of them extremely violent, to judge from the sounds issuing forth.

I think people have grown tired of hearing television blamed for so many social evils, but it seems to be generally accepted that indiscriminate viewing can have a very adverse effect on young children, which certainly seemed to be the case with this little island girl. Within minutes of meeting her, one couldn't miss the fact that her conversation was full of horror; she was an intelligent child, trying to make sense of experiences which she didn't understand and which had left her with unresolved fears. She sat wan-faced at breakfast the next morning, seeking reassurance from her busy mother, that a whole range of ghastly things were not going to happen. I realise there could be many other influences affecting the child, but as the fears she expressed were so specific to what she had seen on television, I was left feeling that more use of the off switch would do one little girl a power of good.

Donald was very shy at first and I was glad there was whisky to help thaw the atmosphere a little. He sat there very upright, with a dram in one hand and his other hand resting on his walking stick. In his dark, old-fashioned clothes and boots he seemed bizarrely out of place in that space-age kitchen, like a character in an historical film who had strayed on to the wrong set. In fact he could well have been involved in the making of *Whisky Galore* and I asked him if he had been. He said he hadn't but that he'd been in the real thing. When the S.S. Politician ran aground, just a few hundred yards off Eriskay's northern shore, Donald had been home on leave from the merchant navy and had had some official position, like ferrying out officials to the wreck and generally keeping an eye on things.

'Mind you,' he said, 'much of it was gone by then, what didn't go to the bottom and get spoilt that is. People came from all over, as far as from the mainland I heard. They came in any sort of boat they could lay their hands on; if it was just the bathtub they had for the journey, I believe they would have come in that. There was no way to stop them, short of shooting them.'

His eyes lit up as he talked about the 'Polly'. It's the one subject that every old island man will talk about for hours. Many of them of course were there and it's not every generation that has the distinction of being present when significant folk-lore history is being made. Had the cargo been anything other than mainly whisky, it would hardly be remembered still, but whisky is what turned it into a living legend. The attitude of island men to drink has much in common with the Vikings of the ancient sagas and remembrance of the 'Polly' conjures up dreams of endless drinking bouts of heroic proportions.

Rumours still circulate that there are caches of bottles all over the hills, the people who hid them there having been too drunk at the time to remember the spot. Others say that the whisky didn't keep at all anyway because the salt water had penetrated the corks and spoilt the contents. One thing however is certain, that the island women in no way shared the men's enthusiasm over the unexpected bounty. Anyone who has seen island men at the end of a real drinking bout could certainly understand why. There is very little opportunity for social drinking, very few pubs and hotels and none at all on some islands. This is probably part of the reason that many of the men drink such vast quantities when they do get the opportunity. But why they seem unable to stop before they are reduced to a state of maudlin helplessness is doubtless a far more complicated matter. I hasten to add that Donald drank his whisky with a most commendable slowness and a lot of water, making two small glasses last the whole evening.

Unlike the Barra seamen I had talked to, Donald had not seemed to develop much of an interest in far places. Seafaring was just a job and he had been far happier at home working on the croft. Most of his time in foreign ports he said, had been spent in trying to find a Catholic Church where he could make his confession and hear mass. I don't think that this was unusual, for even today religion on these small islands has a particularly strong influence and is firmly woven into the social fabric, an everyday thing and not just kept for Sunday.

One story Donald told me illustrated the closeness of the Eriskay community of his day and the sense of responsibility that even a young boy was expected to have towards it. He had been on the sea shore with some friends when he was about nine or ten years old, in a season of spring tides, when the receding water exposed vast areas of the sands and rocks of the treacherous Sound of Barra. The people of Eriskay knew the dangers of those sands and so did all the children, having been warned to keep away from them from the time they could walk. For some reason, Donald and his friends succumbed to temptation on this particular day, one lad egging on another to venture a little further, and a little further until they had wandered far out over the perilous area, nearly as far as the skerries of Lingay. When the tide turns it comes in like an express train, and the boys having left their return too late were caught while still a good distance from the shore and within seconds they were struggling for their lives in the icy water.

That not one of them drowned, Donald puts down to divine intervention, since none of them could swim — I think the reason that on some islands boys did learn to swim and on others they did not was largely due to the presence of a safe bathing place. They had fortunately been spotted from the shore and some men had formed a chain and waded in, up to their necks to haul them out. It was no heroes welcome for the boys, as soon as they had time to get home and into dry clothes the schoolmaster sent for them to administer a beating and it was Donald's misfortune that his dry trousers had a large hole in the seat of them. His mother beat him too, only she waited until the following day. He didn't think the punishment was unkind, or unjust he said, after all he had been fed and cared for for nine years and now he had reached an age where he could be of some use, they were quite right to expect him not to wantonly risk his life. The worst punishment he thought was his own sense of shame that he was nearly drowned through just playing, when so many men had to risk their lives all the time at the fishing. 'Aye,' he said reflectively, 'it took me a good few years to live down that piece of foolishness.'

On a lighter note, he told me of how the very first lorry had come to Eriskay, and had straightaway broken down on the steep unmade island roads; they had to use horses each time to haul the lorry up the hill. I couldn't see why they needed a lorry at all, but apparently the island's shopkeeper had had it brought over to get his stock from the pier to the shop. Now that the E.E.C. have given them a smart new roll on, roll off car ferry, the island is full of cars and lorries, all two square miles of it. I asked him if the horses were the famous Eriskay ponies, but he said there was no such thing, the horses they had were the same as those on the other islands, ordinary Highland ponies, and he doubted if there were more than one or two of those left on the island now — another illusion gone.

The bedding they had used on Eriskay on the other hand might well have been unique. Donald said it was a kind of reed that grew in salt water and was known as sea grass. It had to be renewed every two months or so and when it was first laid on the bed planks, it was built up feet high, so that you needed a chair to climb into bed, but it quickly flattened down and by the time it was replaced it had disintegrated into dust and the occupant was lying on the boards.

Like many of his generation, Donald had built his own house

'with a little help from the stone mason'. I went to see it at his invitation the following morning and found it at the top of a little muddy path, a square, two-storied, solid little house and quite a contrast to my last night's lodgings. His married daughter and her grown children lived with him now, so there were a few concessions to modern convenience, like the washing machine and electric cooker in the scullery but essentially the house was not much different from when Donald had built it forty-five years before. It looked what it was intended to be, a shelter for people whose lives were largely spent out of doors. There were thick walls to keep out the storms but few comforts to encourage idleness. A few hard chairs and a wooden settle, a table and a sideboard were all the furnishings. The floor coverings were linoleum with a runner of threadbare carpet and it must have been a long while since the cream and green paintwork had been renewed. It wasn't elegant certainly, but with a peat fire glowing in the hearth and a blackened kettle gently steaming beside it, it seemed a snug enough retreat from inclement weather.

Before I left, Donald showed me some of the famous Eriskay sweaters, which his daughter had knitted — I was very glad that they at least existed, now that the ponies had proved illusory and even the 'Prince's flowers' were rumoured to be by no means unique to Eriskay. The sweaters were navy blue, shaped very like guernseys, but with a distinctive Celtic pattern which looked at least as ancient as the Book of Kells. These patterns had once all had a symbolic meaning, like runes and were knitted into the garment for the protection of the wearer. Donald said he had always worn such sweaters since childhood and they had always had the same pattern, though some fitted better than others. I could buy one at the Co-op if I wished, though he thought they were asking a terrible price for them.

I did go to the Co-op, because apart from the church there wasn't any other building of significance to visit and both church and shop were centres of island life. I was very impressed with the shop, a spacious new building, with a hall and cafeteria attached; set up as an island co-operative scheme with a grant from the Development Board. The stock was extensive and of much better quality than I had previously seen in other island shops. The sweaters were excellent and for all the work in them, they didn't seem too expensive; I was told by the young girl at the checkout, that they were sold mostly by mail order. Afterwards I visited the church which is a severe looking, grey, granite building set on a small prominence overlooking the harbour. The interior too is more austere than is usual for a Catholic church, but even though it was quite empty, it seemed to have a strong atmosphere of prayer and worship. The altar had as its frontal, the prow of a lifeboat from the Second World War aircraft carrier Hermes and I thought no symbol could have been more appropriate for a congregation whose life was so intimately bound up with the sea and whose menfolk once found their final resting place more often on the sea bed than in the island graveyard.

In the full light of day and without the streaming rain, Eriskay didn't really resemble the Rhondda Valley as I had thought the previous evening. Apart from anything else, the close presence of the sea gave it a grandeur that was entirely absent from the coal-mining village I remembered. Yet a similarity did remain, it was a subtle thing and difficult to pin down but was about a people's struggle with poverty and with an unfruitful soil which had been asked to yield more than it could, so that in the end the land itself had become exhausted and hopeless. It is generally forgotten in an age that looks with horror on the famines in Third World countries that we had our own terrible famines less than 140 years ago, when people died in their thousands throughout Ireland and North West Scotland. Nowhere did they suffer worse than in the Southern half of the Outer Hebrides, owned then by Col. Gordon of Cluny — a man of almost unbelievable callousness. On Eriskay at the peak of the disaster in 1847, the inhabitants had been reduced to eating grass. For people like Donald MacKinnis those times are a living tradition, passed on to them by grandparents and great grand parents who had lived through them. Perhaps it is something of this bitter heritage that makes the visible similarities to the habitats of other oppressed and exploited peoples.

Coilleag a Phrionssa, the Prince's strand is half way along the western shore of Eriskay and is of the same fine white sand as a hundred beaches on other islands. On Eriskay such a beach is especially beautiful because the rest of the island is so rough, and rocky. The Prince's ship had come in here only in order to escape the attentions of another ship which they feared (wrongly) might be English. Lord Boisdale was summoned from South Uist to greet the Prince and he tried hard to persuade the young man to abandon his venture and return home. Had he done so, many of the islanders would not have lost their lives in the bloody battles that followed. There wouldn't have been the horrible reprisals either when hundreds of Highlanders were taken down to London to public execution as a warning to other Jacobites. Hundreds of young men who barely knew why they had been fighting were hung, drawn and quartered at Smithfield, while hundreds more rotted on hulks in the Thames, till death released them and their emaciated bodies were flung into the river – which is the theme of the famous song The Banks of Loch Lomond, so beloved by the Victorians as a sentimental love song, but composed to commemorate those executions. The 'high road' was death on the gibbet and the 'low road' was death by drowning. It was the souls of the executed men returning home who were to meet (or not) on 'the bonny, bonny banks of Loch Lomond'.

Even so, loyalty to the Jacobite cause, or at least to the person of the Prince Charles Edward Stuart never wavered in these islands and in all the months after Culloden, when the Prince was hunted up and down the Outer Hebrides with a tremendous price on his head, no-one seems to have even considered turning him over to the English.

I rode through the rest of the island's roads and tracks and in all the two miles and a bit of scattered housing it seemed to me that there was no shortage of money now on Eriskay. The same fever of building and improving was everywhere apparent; gable ends being raised to add an extra floor; extensions here, a new bungalow there, new porches, windows and skylights everywhere and of course the familiar incongruous 20th century Georgian door. A builder up here should be making his fortune I thought, though tradesmen in fact are as rare as gold. Curiously I saw no people about during my amble through the island and apart from Donald and the girl at the Co-op, I'd talked to no-one, perhaps the men were out fishing and the women busy with housework; no-one certainly was wrestling with the soil.

I left on the one o'clock ferry, I hadn't wanted to stay longer. Eriskay certainly hadn't had anything like the attraction my imagination had imbued it with and although I had anticipated that, perversely, I still felt as though I'd been robbed of something precious. Some weeks later, when I was on a quite a different island, I saw a film about Eriskay which restored more than I had lost on the visit. It had been made by a rich German Count who had been sailing his yacht around the Outer Hebrides in the 1930s and being a keen amateur film-maker, he had filmed the people of Eriskay going about their daily tasks. Where I had seen an island, with almost no-one about, this film showed the same setting filled with island people living a rich communal existence. There certainly wasn't much evidence of wealth or ease, but there were no obvious signs of privation either. They looked a hardy race, demonstrating their traditional skills with a touch of pride. Some of them seemed surprised that they should prove important enough to be taken so much notice of. As they 'waulked' the tweed, carried home the peats, worked at the fishing and performed the hundred-and-one varied tasks that made up their days, the rhythm of the work emerged. The traditional songs that had accompanied those tasks of group effort and had always seemed so odd performed on a concert stage, made sense in this living context. With so much co-operation and shared effort needed for daily existence, it was impossible to imagine modern ills like loneliness and boredom. It was a truly remarkable film, a document made entirely without sentimentality about a way of life that had vanished before its value was ever fully realised.

SEVEN

I am not ignorant that foreigners, sailing through the Western Isles, have been tempted from the sight of so many wild hills, to imagine that the inhabitants as well as the places of their residence, are barbarous. But the lion is not so fierce as he is painted, nor are the people described here so barbarous as the world imagines.

Martin Martin

AFTER ERISKAY I FELT I WANTED TO get right away by myself for a while, hankering after the solitude I'd grown used to at my Barra camp site. In contrast to that, the last few days had been a riot of entertainment. I had had enough of houses for a while and was eager to sleep under the stars again, as long as it stayed dry that is. Accordingly when the ferry unshipped me at Ludag on South Uist, I turned my back on the road and headed for South Glendale and a rough track which led northwards over a shoulder of a low hill called Maraval. South Glendale was miles from anywhere, just a few houses and a handful of fields, tucked into a fold of grey-green hills. I remembered that Elizabeth had told me that she had taught here and on Eriskay before she married and had been desperate with homesickness the whole time, even though there had been endless ceilidhs and dances. She'd asked me to give Glendale her love if I passed by. Remembering this I thought I would at least look at the scene of her labours and I asked an old woman who had come out onto the doorstep of her stone bungalow, where the school was. She said it had gone years past but had been at the meeting of the tracks, two miles on, over the hill. 'They built it there to be central for all the scholars coming from North Glendale and South Glendale. Later we asked for our own school, but there are no scholars here now and if there were, the bus would be taking them to Daliburgh.'

I would have liked to ask her more about the changes in her remote village but knew that if I did she would invite me in and make me a 'strupak' — tea and sandwiches, scones and whatever else was in the house, for such hospitality is still the norm towards strangers in places like that, and to refuse would be churlish. I didn't want to impose on her generosity however and so I thanked her for the information and rode on up the stony track.

It was great fun riding Evans on the sort of terrain he was designed for, although he was rather too overladen to really show his paces to the full and where the track broke into deep ruts, the front panniers kept catching on the sides, all but unseating me. Nevertheless it was a lot easier, even where I had to get off and push, than walking and carrying all that luggage on my back. After I'd crossed the shoulder of Maraval it was impossible to ride even on the Tank's fat tyres for the track descended through increasingly boggy ground, where the waters running down from a high mountain loch spread out into the surrounding peat until finally even a trace of the path disappeared altogether. Evans sank in up to his axles and I dithered about from tussock to peat hag, trying to stay dryshod. Once I'd given up this futile attempt, I got along more easily, though by the time I'd joined up with the east-west track, I was soaked to well above the knees and wished I'd thought to remove my footwear and roll up my trousers.

I had not really planned where I was going, but thought I would camp soon, at the first likely spot. Eastward led back towards Loch Boisdale and civilization; westward, the map showed the track running on for about four miles through uninhabited country to end abruptly at the sea, with not even a ruin indicated along its entire length. I turned west, not with the intention of going to the end of the track but just to see where I should get to. A green path stretching away into the unknown is an invitation hard to resist and I have seldom regretted following where such a way leads, but on this particular day I had grave doubts about my choice for a long while.

I wandered on looking for a likely spot to make camp. The day had turned overcast and a little drizzly, which didn't make any-where look particularly appealing, and there was no apparent dry spot anywhere to pitch even as small a tent as mine. The flat valley bottom through which the road ran was a depressing place, a water-logged barren wilderness of greyish green herbage, with bog cotton dotted about in peat-stained surface water. Sometimes my boot

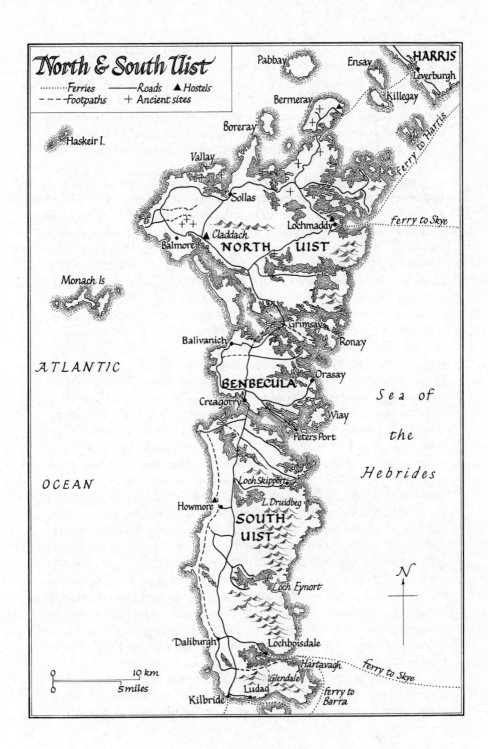

North & South Uist

...... Ferries ——— Roads ▲ Hostels
- - - - Footpaths + Ancient sites

HARRIS
Pabbay
Ensay
Leverburgh
Bermeray
Killegay
Boreray
ferry to Harris
Haskeir I.
Vallay
Sollas
ferry to Skye
Lochmaddy
Claddach
NORTH UIST
Balmore
Monach Is
Grimsay
Balivanich
Ronay
ATLANTIC
BENBECULA
Orasay
Creagorry
Wiay
Peters Port
OCEAN
Sea of
the
Hebrides
Loch Skipport
L. Druidbeg
Howmore
SOUTH
UIST
N
Loch Eynort
Daliburgh
Lochboisdale
Hartavagh
ferry to Skye
10 km
Glendale
5 miles
Ludag
ferry to
Barra
Kilbride

would sink in above the ankle and when I drew it out it came away with a squelch and almost immediately the hole filled up with brown water. Probably the area had once been the summer shielings of the people of Glendale, where the women and children took the cattle to in the summer months, staying there with them, making butter and cheese, while the fields around the crofts grew a crop of hay for the winter feeding. If I was right the deterioration of the land since that time was most marked.

Much of the ground would have been green and not nearly so boggy; now even the sheep, the 'white scourge' who had displaced the human occupants seemed to have abandoned it. The finer grasses had been eaten out by the sheep, while the coarser grasses had been left to fill the gaps and the fragile, marginal land had been despoiled. With no-one to put a bit of heart back into it, it was as good as dead. The only hint of flourishing growth in the whole debased glen was the waving bracken on the few low knolls that broke up the flatness and were naturally well-drained. Bracken moves in where ground that was once planted has been abandoned, so these low knolls were the only visible memorial of the former people who had wrested a living here. If I had searched amongst the bracken stems I would probably have found some of the scattered stones of their summer dwellings.

Bordering this valley to the south was a line of long narrow lochs, with dark, wind-ruffled water lapping against the eastern shores with margins of white spume. There were islands in these lochs, covered with thick scrub and heather, one or two even had small trees growing out of the scrub, a great rarity in the Outer Hebrides. Had the sheep been able to get out to these islets, there would have been only the same impoverished growth as in the surrounding landscape. I tried to imagine what the whole area had looked like before the great sheep take-over had occurred, when cattle still grazed the low hills which sheltered the glen to the north, naturally replenishing the earth's fertility; and before the land had been burnt off again and again in an attempt to encourage the regeneration of the grasses favoured by the sheep, which had succeeded only in hastening the land's demise. I found this act of imagination too difficult, the changes were just too great to envisage, as Frank Fraser Darling, an ecologist far ahead of his time had written:

'The coming of the sheep caused a revolution in natural history quite as certainly as it effected the lives of the people and the subsequent history of the people has been quite definitely affected by that revolution in natural history and the new eco-systems it brought about.'

Had I been forced to camp there, the only place would have been on the track itself, for even though it degenerated every so often into the same boggy morass as the land around it, it had plenty of dry patches too, healthily green against the sickly undrained soil. It was a splendid road, although it couldn't have been in use for years. The culverts were mostly clogged or broken and the stone piers which had once supported bridges across the burns, stood useless now, supporting nothing. The quality of the workmanship was still apparent however and it would be many centuries before the last traces of such a road faded, altogether, even if no-one ever used it again. I wondered if it was one of the 'destitution roads', built in the famines of the 1840s by the starving islanders who in return for back-breaking labour, eight hours a day, six days a week were given 'wages' of a subsistence level of grain or oatmeal, for themselves, their wives and any children under twelve. The worth of which on average amounted to rather less than half the lowest wage on the open market of that time.

In some ways the Scots were luckier than the Irish in that the potato blight which brought about the famines happened in Ireland first. The British government had therefore had some opportunity for observing the effects of mass starvation and the attendant cholera, typhoid and dysentry which decimated a weakened people. Accordingly when the blight struck on the Scottish mainland and the islands in 1846, there was an attempt to bring swift relief and only two deaths were ever officially recorded as being solely caused by starvation (those two significantly were on Barra). The thousands of deaths whose primary cause was undoubtedly malnutrition were able to be attributed more acceptably to the accompanying diseases.

Free handouts were certainly not to be thought of, even though a relief fund was set up to administer charitable contributions which had come from as far afield as Canada, where emigrants sent grain, money and even salt beef to help their former kinsmen. As Sir Charles Trevelyan, the Treasury official in charge of the government's aid put it:

'Next to allowing people to die of hunger, the greatest evil that could happen would be their being habituated to depend upon public charity. The object to be arrived at therefore, is to prevent the assistance given from being productive of idleness and if possible, to make it conducive to increased exertion.'

Odd how the Victorians always seemed to equate poverty with inherent indolence and culpable shiftlessness. In order to prevent the evil consequences of charitable handouts a whole army of 're-spectable' people were employed to administer the funds, which meant seeing that a fair day's work was extracted for the exchange of the subsistence level of grain. Emily Macleod, the sister of MacLeod of Dunvegan, one of the few landlords who did help his tenants generously from his own funds, wrote of the iniquity of the system:

'Crofters feel the injustice of being paid at a very low rate out of what they not unnaturally consider their own money and are exas-perated at seeing gentlemen living in comfort on what they know was subscribed for them, while they have to walk, often without shoes and always in insufficient clothing to the source of labour where, after working for eight hours, they receive the value of a penny halfpenny.'

So inadequate was the allowance that there were reports of workers collapsing on the roads they were constructing, a fact cor-roborated by the Board's inspectors, one of whom wrote:

'The people are very willing to work but so much are they weak-ened by insufficient food that much work cannot be got out of them.'

On Col. Gordon's Outer Hebridean estate of Benbecula, South Uist, Barra and the smaller islands in between, like Eriskay, the pre-dicament of the crofters was worse than anywhere, but Gordon, an absentee landlord was prepared to do little if anything for his tenants. It wasn't until the Treasury official wrote him an extremely fiery letter, threatening to go over his head to alleviate the suffering and then let Parliament decide on who should foot the bill, that Gordon took up his option on government aided improvement schemes. Roads and drainage schemes were on the face of things a very good idea, especially as they were costing the landlords nothing. If only they could have been planned so as to benefit the crofters' holdings, some of their future sufferings might have been avoided, but as so often has been the case with the administering of charitable schemes, little of the benefit actually helped the people it was intended for.

The people who were dying all over Col. Gordon's estate were in any case a redundant population by this stage in their history and Gordon like his fellow land owners was only too keen to get rid of them and turn their holdings over to sheep. This was due to an ironic twist of circumstances. Fifty years before it was the people themselves who were eager to leave their ancestral homes and make a new life for themselves in the colonies. For towards the end of the 18th Century, as the tide of sheep began to sweep inexorably over ever vaster tracks of land, whole communities had chosen to take their chances abroad, rather than submit to being hounded into the newly set-up crofting townships. Sheep farming at that time however was not the sole method of obtaining the maximum cash return from Hebridean estates, there was also an even more lucrative commodity, called kelp.

Kelp was invaluable as a source of industrial alkali for use in glass and soap works and was in increasing demand as those industries grew. A rival and much cheaper source, called barilla was imported from Spain, but this was cut off after 1790, when French military activity began to affect trade in Europe. In consequence the price of kelp rocketed until it became the principal source of income in places like South Uist, where between 1801-1802 the estate realised £9,454 from kelp and £5,297 from land rents i.e. sheep farms. Kelp was made from the seaweed growing in great abundance on the Atlantic shores of North Western Scotland, particularly on the Outer Hebrides. The seaweed was cut, dried and then incinerated in shallow pits. Its supply was virtually limitless and so a vast army of men, women and children were needed in order to reap the maximum profits. Kelping seems to have been a particularly nasty occupation made worse by brutish conditions, about which one 18th century traveller commented, 'The life of a negro slave on the plantations is paradise compared to that of a Hebridean kelper.' Another traveller remarked that a 'pall of nauseous smoke hung over the scene of their labours, for all of the Summer months, stretching from Barra in the south to Lewis in the north and visible far out to sea'. Clearly it was no sinecure and in order to prevent the profitable workforce from leaving *en masse* for greener pastures on the other side of the Atlantic, special Parliamentary legislation was hurriedly passed, which increased the passage fare to the colonies threefold and thus prevented the incipient wholesale emigration.

With the whole population now herded into small townships and paying rent to their landlord, who also controlled the kelp industry and fixed the desperately low wages, a system of exploitation existed as vicious as any in the factories or mines of industrial England. The only way the population could obtain enough food on their diminished holdings was by concentrating on potatoes, which by 1811 was reckoned to constitute over 80 per cent of the diet. The population grew steadily during the twenty or so years of the kelp boom, becoming hopelessly overcrowded and totally dependent upon their one crop.

By the 1820s when the bottom had dropped out of the kelp market, due to the return of the much cheaper barilla, the only way for land owners to make good some of their lost revenues was to take over the already reduced holdings of the small tenants and rent them out to the sheep farmers, who would pay at least double for the same land. Wool was needed in ever greater quantities for the Northern mills and mutton was needed to feed the populations of the growing Southern towns. People were no longer the 'islands' wealth'; they had become a 'drain on resources' and must be removed to make way for the sheep. On South Uist and Benbecula it was decided that half the population, some 3000 people would have to be shipped to America — 'shovel out the paupers' became acceptable policy. The few who could afford it went independently, but until the island was bought by the wealthy Gordon of Cluny in 1841 there were not enough funds available to tackle the wholesale enforced shipment of so many people.

In all the awful chronicles of the Highland Clearances there have been none that quite matched the brutality of those carried out on Col. Gordon's estate. Desperately impoverished and misused though they were the island people were deeply attached to their homes and they had to be forcibly removed from them. Roofs were burnt over their heads and folk fleeing to the hills were hunted down with the aid of dogs, bound and forced onto the ships that Gordon had chartered. A young girl, Catherine MacPhee who lived at Iochdar on South Uist, left this eye witness account of the events:

'Many a thing have I seen in my own day and generation. Many a thing, O Mary Mother of the black sorrow. I have seen the townships swept, and the big holdings being made of them, the people being driven out of the countryside to the streets of Glasgow and to the wilds of Canada, such of them that did not die of hunger and plague and smallpox while going across the ocean. I have seen the women putting the children in the carts which were being sent from Benbecula and the Iochdar to Loch Boisdale, while their husbands lay bound in the pen and were weeping beside them, without power to give them a helping hand, though the women themselves were crying aloud and their little children were wailing to break their hearts. I have seen the big strong men, the champions of the countryside, being bound on Loch Boisdale quay and cast into the ship as would be done to a batch of horses or cattle, the bailiffs and the ground-officers and the constables and the policemen gathered behind them in pursuit of them. The God of life and He only knows all the loathsome works of men on that day.'

Gordon's unfortunate ex-tenants, who survived the transportation were dumped, totally destitute, some without even clothes to their backs, upon the quays of Quebec harbour. Representations were made to him, both by his peers at home and by the Canadian authorities, to provide some means of giving the wretched people a start in their new country. Most of the other landlords had done at least this much, however badly they had behaved towards their tenants in other respects. Gordon categorically refused, his response being that he was 'neither legally nor morally bound to support a population made destitute by the will of Providence'.

I was moving through the very countryside where these incidents had taken place, Loch Boisdale which had witnessed the terrible scenes described by Catherine MacPhee was just over the hill to the north, a few miles away. So it was not unnatural that the dark deeds of that tragic past should seem to hang around this valley. Once I had passed the last of the long black lochs however, the mood of the day changed and things improved. Most importantly, the sun came out and that altered the whole aspect of the land straight away. Everywhere looks better in sunshine, but this is especially the case in the Outer Hebrides. I think its because the colours are so delicate and the contrasts so slight and subtle, that without a strong, warm light, everything looks lifeless. Once the sky has cleared, its intense northern blueness adds a sheen to everything else and with so much moisture about, on the ground and in the air, the blueness is reflected from a hundred, thousand sources. The air itself seems to dance with tiny motes of colour.

After I had laboriously forded another six-foot wide burn, dryshod, but badly scraping Evan's paintwork on the boulders, I came to a gate. It stood there squarely across the path but of the wire fencing on either side of it, there was no trace, it must have quite rusted away over the years, whereas the gate being galvanised looked as good as new. I would have stepped off the path and walked around it had the ground not been particularly boggy just there. I pushed the gate experimentally and it fell down, its supports coming away with it in one piece.

The gate I realised later had marked the boundary of a crofting township, the township of Bay Hartavagh, so remotely placed and long-forgotten that even the Ordnance Survey hadn't marked its remaining ruins. The surroundings had altered the moment I'd stepped over the fallen gate which at first I'd put down to the effect of the sun, but soon realised that it was more than that. There was a slight but definite improvement in the quality of the soil and a wider variety of grasses and plants grew. There was plenty of heather and six or seven different wild flowers were visible on and around the path — small, low-growing species, like selfheal, eyebright, wild thyme and birdsfoot trefoil, and there were small lochans dotted about, their surfaces covered with big, round, flat, green leaves, through which the white, waxy heads of water lilies rose and opened to the warmth of the sun. These natural lily ponds are exquisite and would grace the finest garden; no matter how often I come across them their voluptuousness still seem unbelievably exotic in such wild places.

Soon the track began to descend steeply and the burn I had forded earlier came tumbling down a little gorge on my right, to pass again across the track. A little way up this gorge, on the edge of the burn was a ruin, just one standing wall and a few courses of massive, roughly-dressed stone. It stood in a sheltered spot and a few rare saplings grew against it; it could have been a mill, for it was in the right position for one and the flow of water was enough to turn a wheel, also the dimensions were rather larger than I would expect for an ordinary dwelling. It seemed amazingly domestic and vulnerable in that rough wilderness. Ahead I could see another smaller ruin on a steep hillside surrounded by a sea of bracken. When I reached this, the sea came into view below and I was looking down on a narrow, fiord-like bay, opening to the north, with a small island near its landward end and further islands beyond. The track clearly descended and continued right around to the far side of the bay, where I could make out more roofless ruins. I found the first sight of this lonely, long-abandoned settlement, strangely moving; that a viable existence had been established in so wild and remote a place seemed little short of miraculous, that it had proved no longer tenable, after the immense labour that must have gone into its making, seemed nothing short of tragic.

I went on with some difficulty as the track curved around a hill-side thick with bracken, which had obscured the path and whose tough stems caught in all of Evan's projecting parts. As if to compensate, the scenery became ever more beautiful with each step I took. Two more burns, without bridges passed twenty feet or so

Callanish, Lewis

Lewis

Marion Campbell, Prockapool, Harris

Stockinish, Harris

Stockinish, Harris

Restored black house, Lewis

North Uist

Stornoway

Stornoway

Ancient Cross, North Uist

South Uist

Harris

Standing stone on the machair, Harris

Ancient Cross, North Uist

South Uist

Vatersay

Vatersay

Howmore, South Uist

Uig, Lewis

Harris

Standing stone on the machair, Harris

below the track, so that I had to clamber down, ford them and drag Evans up the other side; feats made easier by first throwing all four panniers across the gaps to lighten the load. Wherever there was a flat space, big enough for a dwelling, I could see on it a squat, man-made rectangle of stone amid the sea of luxuriant bracken; there were no more than half a dozen of these, so rough and precipitous was the ground. One was a more substantial ruin than the others, but still no more than a two roomed stone dwelling with the walls built up a little and a sheet of corrugated iron weighted down with stones over one corner of it. It appeared to be used as a make-shift sheep-pen, by present day shepherds and had a fenced area in front of it, covered with the marks of small sharp hooves. A roughly con-trived sheep dip stood in one corner and tins of chemicals and empty whisky bottles and beer cans in another.

I continued on down to the level of the sea, feeling so immeasur-ably happy in the surroundings and the sunshine that I sang as I went and disturbed two herons, who rose up like the two halves of a single grey umbrella and made off across the bay with slow deliber-ate wingbeats. From the island, which I could now see was an island only at high tide, a single file of recently clipped sheep made their way across the stony beach, heading back towards the track before the tide turned. In the shelter of the island — Eilean Dubh (the Black Island) I felt that I had reached the centre of the old settlement. There were one or two well separated ruins, each standing on the very fringe of the high water mark so as to leave the maximum amount of land behind for growing crops. The furrows left by the old lazybeds showed up in sharp detail in the shadows cast by the sun, slowly descending now over the glen I had walked through. Low hills enclosed it completely except for the narrow cleft of the bay. It was a most beautiful place but terrible too and one could only marvel at the fortitude of people who had sustained life here. Nowhere was there a flat piece of ground, or a dry one as I dis-covered when I looked around for a place to pitch the tent. The soil was just a thin layer over impervious rock, boggy and poor, with old drainage ditches criss-crossing it, desperately close together. Every inch of ground had been utilised and even so there was precious little for the two dozen or so families who appeared to have lived here. The best thing about it was the closeness of the sea and the sheltered bay where a boat would lie safely at all points of the wind. Clearly it had been a community almost wholly dependent upon the sea.

I pitched my small green tent within the walls of the most attractively placed ruin and set up camp there, for it was the only dry flat area I could find. The sheep use these old ruins for shelter, wherever they occur and over the years their droppings have mixed with the rubble and earth, creating a flat, even surface over which a good turf usually establishes itself. All that was needed to make this one ideal, was a quick sweep out of the recent droppings with a clump of heather. With the one-man tent erected, I was left with a small space at the gable end where the opening of the old fireplace made a homely spot to set out the cooking things. The walls of my shelter were massive and marvellously constructed out of huge unhewn stones and boulders, the interstices filled with scraps of rock. They stood at about six feet, the original height probably, on the broad flat top of which the thatch had once rested, supported on any driftwood that could serve as rafters and weighted down with nets fringed with heavy stones. Two window spaces gave me a view up the little fiord to the sea and as I sat on one of the broad sills, sipping a well-earned whisky, I saw the car ferry going past the narrow exit at what seemed a tremendous speed, making for Loch Boisdale and civilization. I felt very happy to be where I was.

The whole settlement took very little time to explore. The best land was on Eilean Dubh, where the old lazybeds were covered in good turf and thick heather. The biggest single building work, apart from the road, seemed to have been the clearing of the foreshore of rocks and stones; across this cleared area, the sheep had beaten a well-defined path on their trips to graze on the island. Behind the low hills at the back of the settlement were several quite small lochs, separated by narrow strips of ground, which drained down to the bay and these burns appeared to have been the only source of domestic water for the village, at least I found no wells or springs. There were more old lazybeds in amongst these lochans, on any patch of ground that offered a purchase for them and at some distance beyond these, on the higher slopes, I came upon their peat banks.

My explorations were made somewhat difficult by the continual attacks I suffered from a large, belligerent herring gull. This bird took up a position on a knob of land in the bay, about eighty yards from my camp and every time I appeared outside, he would fly straight at me, making for my head and sheering away only at the very last moment. I have been similarly attacked by the huge Arctic skuas on St. Kilda, when I have strayed into their breeding grounds. The skuas are masters of the art of parting a person's hair while just avoiding actual impact. They climb to quite a height before attacking so that the speed at which they come at one creates a slip stream and had they talons instead of webbed feet, I think they would be lethal. Their attacks made this lesser bully seem more comical than alarming. Nor did I discover the reason for his aggression since it was well past the breeding season and there were no nests around that I could see. I decided in the end that he had developed an inflated notion of his territorial rights and was set on a career of land-grabbing like the Victorians before him. When the herons returned later to stalk the tideline, he slunk off.

After I'd seen all there was of the village and its surroundings, I sat for ages at the threshold of the house, watching the tide come in under the changing colours of the evening sky. It was almost the longest day, when the light in these northern latitudes merges imperceptively into a half darkness, before slowing flooding again into full daylight. On this evening the sun made his brief disappearance with a glory I have never seen equalled. The clear, radiant blue softened down further and further until it was difficult to say whether it was still blue or pale primrose. Across this luminous background, wisps of clouds caught the reflection of the invisible sun in shades of soft creamy pinks, orange and deep fiery red. A few late evening birds crossed the bay with an occasional wild call and the tide murmured on the shingle and I thought that this was probably as close to perfection as I had ever been.

Later when it was dark, I made a small fire of dead heather roots, in the fireplace of the ruin and sat on a stone beside it thinking, inevitably I suppose, about the former inhabitants. On one side of what had been the hearth was a patch of nettles; I had cooked some of them to eat with my supper of potatoes and cheese. Young nettles are supposed to be a good substitute for spinach, but I had cooked them more in a spirit of accepting the hospitality of the place. I felt rather like a guest, for there was such a strong feeling of other people around. It wasn't at all a ghostly feeling, rather the reverse really and it certainly didn't have me nervously looking over my shoulder. Before I turned in, I placed Evans across the empty doorway to keep out any sheep who might otherwise stray in and get tangled in the guy ropes. Then I lay down in my sleeping bag, with the strongest feeling of being benignly watched over and slept unusually deeply and well, until far into the next morning.

EIGHT

Northwart fra thir Iles forsaid, lyes the grate Ile of
Ywst, 34 myles lang from the south south-west to the
north north-eist, sex myles braid, ane fertile countrie,
full of heigh hills.

Dean Munro

PETERANNA IS NO GAELIC NAME, EVEN
with Shamus tacked on in front, but this is what the most enterprising man I met in South Uist was called. Shamus Peteranna had
appeared at my side one day like an angel fulfilling wishes. It was a
perfectly vile day with a gale-force north wind blowing straight off
the Arctic ice, cold enough to bite to the bone even through several
layers of woollens and windproof clothing. It was the sort of day
when a bicyclist should either be scudding along before the wind,
like a sailing ship running free, or else firmly under cover. I had had
my free passage earlier in the day, covering twelve wildly exhilarating miles in less than half an hour, the pedals motionless most of the
time and Evan's fat tyres singing on the tarmac like an Aboriginal's
bullroarer.

I had been to consult a local sage who was reputed to be very
knowledgeable about island history and whom I hoped would be
able to tell me something about the old settlement at Bay Hartavagh. He was a kindly old man, eager to help but his subject was
Gaelic patronymics and involved South Uist genealogies. Of Bay
Hartavagh he knew nothing at all and had never been there,
although it was only six miles as the crow flies from where he had
lived all his life. He was most reluctant however to let me go away
none the wiser and I had spent a frustrating afternoon trying not to
go to sleep by the warm fireside, while he droned on and on about
'mics' and 'macs' and other Gaelic prefixes, quite incomprehensible

to me. His wife who unashamedly kept nodding off, had awoken every little while to offer more tea and to say, 'Whist now Angus, the lady doesn't want to be hearing about all that.'

Now that I was on my way back to Howmore where I was based, struggling into the teeth of the gale, the wind had if anything increased in strength and was driving before it a horizontal blanket of ice-cold rain. There was no question of the one good foot being able to do the work of two in these conditions and the damaged one had not been improved by the recent cross-country activity. Even with two good feet I would probably have ended up walking back and I had been practically forced to a standstill by a particularly malevolent blast, when a blue van pulled up beside me. In spite of the 'Uist Builders' painted on the side of it and the dark, foreign looking man who slid open the door to speak to me, I was convinced that it was another instance of the Hand of Providence intervening in an hour of need — like Elijah's chariot of fire. The man however spoke in the normal soft island accent — 'It's a wild day for that sort of work. Will I put the bike in the back for you, I've plenty room?'

Even before he introduced himself as Shamus Peteranna, I thought he couldn't be of island stock with such a pronounced Mediterranean cast of features. Nor were his name and his looks his only unusual attributes. Subsequently I had several conversations with him at Howmore when he came to look over his small herd of cows and I came to think that his nature owed far more to the foreign strain in him than to the island side. There was a tautness about him, a sense of limitless energy and enthusiasm, qualities not necessarily absent from islanders, but certainly not so immediately discernable. Where Hebrideans exhude a sense of infinite time and 'Och there's no hurry' is a favourite expression, Shamus Peteranna seemed like a coiled spring.

His great-grandfather had been a Portuguese ship's carpenter, shipwrecked on the coast of Barra in the 18th century. Whilst waiting for a passage home he had turned his hand to a bit of joinery, by way of repaying the people who were looking after him and he found that his skill was much sought after. Repatriation had been a long time coming and in the meantime he had had a chance to get to know the people and decided that he liked both them and their islands and had decided to stay. His first name, Louis was simple enough but his surname had probably been too difficult and the Peteranna was probably a combination of his parents Christian names. Eventually he moved to South Uist, married and thrived, producing four sons, all of whom were taught a different trade. The tradition of craftsmanship had been maintained and Shamus ran a general building firm, the only one in the Uists I believe.

'I could give a job to everyone who applied. I never have enough men for the work that's there,' he told me. I found this a novel concept in an area where unemployment is said to be second only to depopulation as the current social problem. He thought that the reason for this chronic labour shortage was a sort of malaise that was everywhere in the islands and probably had much to do with a history that had ground people down until it had destroyed their initiative, so that they didn't really want to work anymore. He said it was the same with the crofts, it didn't really pay many of them to work their land when they were given government money for leaving it unworked — the difference in income was too slight. They were attached to their land but no longer had any confidence in what to do with it. 'They think I'm daft to bother with cows and they don't understand that its a pleasure for me, a hobby if you like. The business gives me a good living but without the cows, and coming up here to tend them, I might as well be on the mainland.' I asked what affect he thought the television had had on island life. 'A disaster,' he said. 'It's like a poison and it's finished the social life of the island. With the radio you'd get people turning it off when they'd had enough but they'll stare at that box until their eyes drop out. It would take the house going on fire to get them away from it.'

He had an aggressively new, large bungalow near Daliburgh which looked as though it would be full of electric gadgetry. It seemed to be run as a cross between a guest house and a B&B and I doubt he lost money on the cattle either. He was the sort of man to whom material success came naturally, leaving much of his store of energy untapped and I think it was very fortunate for him that he had such an active and conscious delight in the outdoor world of the islands which could absorb some of the residue. He had been away from the island, both at school and gaining his early experience in the building trade and was in a position to compare values and life-styles. For him island life won hands down, even though he was aware of how fast its values were changing. For as he said, 'Things are changing, everywhere's the same; the whole world is going mad, with the arms race on one hand and half the world starving. At least here everyone knows everyone else and that's important. It isn't until you go away that you realise how important it is, and it's not just that there are no robberies and muggings and murders. It's more knowing you belong somewhere. No matter what happens, it will always be better here and I doubt they'll manage to ruin South Uist in my lifetime.'

About tourism his ideas were mixed, on the one hand he thought the future of the island must lie with catering for visitors and that more should be done to encourage the tourist industry. On the other hand he didn't relish the changes large numbers of tourists could make on the environment. If tourism grew to any extent he felt that remoter parts of the island would have to be made access-ible by building more roads. It was he who first pointed out to me how limited an idea of South Uist is gained by visitors who simply drive through from Loch Maddy in North Uist to pick up the ferry again at Loch Boisdale. 'I'm torn two ways about it,' he said, 'I don't know whether to be glad because it keeps the place unspoilt or sorry that South Uist isn't more appreciated, as it deserves to be.'

South Uist does indeed guard its secrets more securely than the other large islands in the chain. I'm sure Shamus Peteranna is right when he says this is because there is just the one main road which begins at the Loch Boisdale ferry and runs up northwards through the middle of the island to the causeways that join South Uist to Benbecula and Benbecula to North Uist. The eastern side is approached by road only at four points. These single-track roads give no more than a glimpse of the highly convoluted terrain, before ending abruptly at the head of the sea lochs which cut deeply into the land. Once these lochs were full of fishing boats; steamers carrying mixed cargoes put in at jetties which have now almost mouldered away. In what were substantial townships only a house or two still has a roof and peat smoke coming from the chimneys.

To see anything of this rocky eastern side, with its hidden glens and hill lochs and its miles of wild coastline, riven with secret coves, which only seabirds, hawks and seals frequent, means going on foot. With care and a good pair of boots it is wonderful walking country, endlessly varied and surprising. Even when people lived here in the fertile glens, and the hillsides were dotted with their summer shiel-ings, before the whole place was turned over, first to the sheep and later to sporting interests, much of it must have been essentially a lonely and beautiful wilderness. Bonny Prince Charlie spent many nights holed up in its rocky fastnesses, evading the Redcoats and keeping the cold at bay with 'strong spirits' — doubtless taking the edge off his sense of failure at the same time and also laying the foundation for his future alcoholism.

It's the country between Loch Skipport and Loch Einort that I especially enjoy, because here are the Dean's 'Heigh Hills' — Ben More, Ben Corrodale and Hecla, and treading these airy ridges gives one a sensation of elevation and detachment quite out of proportion to the actual height of them. There is nothing to establish a scale, nothing to diminish or to relate to, one is simply high above a slender thread of island with a panorama of ocean, so vast that it seems like being on a different plane of existence. Scotland is the sort of place where memorable views occur too frequently to be retained in much detail, they tend to merge into a general composite of sea, sky and mountains. But there are two or three outlooks so breathtakingly particular, that they remain separate in the mind's eye ever afterwards. One is the view westward from the Cuillin Ridge on Skye with the long line of the Outer Hebrides like a grey whisper in the middle distance and the tangle of the islands of the Inner Hebrides in the foreground. Whenever I stand on Hecla and look east toward Skye, I remember that view with such vividness that I have the odd sensation of having climbed into the canvas of a landscape to see the same view from the other side. Even more memorable is the view westward from this high point in South Uist, especially at evening when the sun is low and there is a beckoning golden road across an ocean that appears to go on for ever. Throughout history this western prospect fascinated the imagination of the people who lived here and excited speculation and dreams, so that a folklore evolved about Tir Nan Og — islands of eternal youth and blessedness, just beyond the far horizon, at the end of the golden path. A different but no less romantic dream called St. Brendan and all that race of Celtic sailor-monks, setting off north and west in their fragile curraghs — converting, praying, fasting and endlessly exploring from island to island until they finally reached America, several centuries before those other indefatigable sea travellers, the Vikings are thought to have stumbled upon the same far coasts.

What draws me most in this western view is the small, high island that lies fifty miles out, a place which once visited leaves an indelible impression on the mind ever afterwards. This is St. Kilda and is actually several separate small islands, though most of them are just huge rock fangs rising from the sea like prehistoric monsters, their upper portions white with the droppings of the gannets who breed there. The main island Hirta is less than a mile across but so high that it makes its own weather, so that there is always a cloud about it either picking up or letting go its moisture — the cloud is the first glimpse one catches of the island from the sea, that or the myriad flocks of birds that circle it. In some respects it is a frightening island with its immense sheer cliffs — the highest in Britain, its stony barrenness and its awful isolation — a mere speck in all those wastes of ocean. But it sustained human life in unbroken succession for thousands of years and what reports exist of that civilization show a contented, healthy people with probably more peace of mind than most of us enjoy.

When I first landed there some years ago, I straight away rushed up to the top of Oiseval, eager to get my first view of the famous cliffs and just as I was reaching the summit a fulmar suddenly appeared at face height, hanging in the air just in front of me. The shock of this sight brought me abruptly and quite literally to my knees — which was just as well for I was on the edge of a vertical thirteen hundred foot drop. Lying full length and peering over I could hear the sea below thundering and booming but it was so far below, that with the thin sea mist that was running I couldn't see the surface. Needles of rock and rough stacks jutted upwards from somewhere near the base of the cliffs, huge things but dwarfed by the distance and changing shape as the mist swirled and eddied. I lay there shaken by the savagery of the scene and thinking of Dean Munro's words about St. Kilda 'the seas about are stark and verie evill'. Later I spent hours in the same spot, watching that most marvellous of all flying wonders — fulmars sporting on the complicated air currents, like so many skiers bending and turning and crossing each others' paths, inches from the rock and hanging there for that one motionless second at the summit, before beginning the whole thing over again, but I never quite lost the sense of fear of the cliffs which I'd felt that first day.

In the two weeks I was on St. Kilda, I stayed with some others in the old village, abandoned when the people were so tragically evacuated thirty years earlier. We were a working party helping to restore some of the buildings as a memorial to those last inhabitants, and to the thousands of years of unbroken habitation. Most of us had come because we were addicted to islands and this was the ultimate in island experiences. Others were keen naturalists, for there are unique birds there too, like the St. Kilda wren and Leach's fork-tailed petrels that come out only at night and dart about for hours like bats, uttering strange, high-pitched cries. But what I remember most about being out there was the constant sense of overwhelming vulnerability and of man's feebleness amid all those overwhelming natural forces, and at the same time of feeling sustained and protected. It engendered a rather child-like state of trust and I was not alone amongst the group in feeling this, in fact nearly everyone there admitted to experiencing something similar. Someone described it as like 'being held in the hand of God'. Whether it was our own response to being in so wild a place or whether we were picking up something in the atmosphere, of the strong religious faith of the former islanders I don't know, but it was the core of my St. Kilda experience and looking at the lovely shape of the island from the summit of Hecla I always feel a wrench as though I've lost something valuable which I knew only for those two weeks.

In total contrast to the rough, high ground of the east, the western seaboard of South Uist presents the gentlest of pastoral aspects, at least in summer. A mile-wide strip of undulating, fertile machair stretches the entire length of the island, beside an unbroken margin of pure, white shell sand. This is the wealth of South Uist where beef cattle are raised and crops grown. All of the island's 2,500 inhabitants live on this machair, apart from the three hundred or so who are on the crofts scattered about the rough ground around Loch Boisdale. Even so South Uist appears extraordinarily empty compared with Barra — which itself could hardly claim to be overcrowded. Most of the land is open grazing, with a few planted fields around the small townships and there is even a golf course — something which must surely have been invented here, so naturally does the terrain fit it. The close-cropped, springy turf makes perfect fairways and greens, without any expensive landscaping, and bunkers occur wherever a localised spot of erosion exposes the underlying sand. As far as I can see only flags and the little holes in the centre of the greens are necessary additions. If I were a golfer I am sure it would be my favourite course, so liberally is it carpeted with wild flowers and under so intensely blue a sky. Talking with some of the players in the bar at Daliburgh however, I gathered that it was not as idyllic as appeared at first sight; for rabbits are so prolific that they are undermining the fairways and golf balls are disappearing in huge numbers down their burrows.

The walker or bicyclist can travel the whole length of this western plain, on the small roads and tracks which serve the villages and gain an intimate glimpse of the crofting life of the island. It is even possible to walk or cycle the entire way in total solitude, keeping close to the unending, pristine beach along the line of the dunes, and for the one, two or three days that it takes, see only rabbits scuttling down holes and bold, inquisitive steers bunching together behind the safety of a few wire strands, to inspect the passing stranger. From this sea-dominated, flower-strewn plain the other side of the island is just an occasionally glimpsed backdrop of far blue hills.

From the main road a third impression is gained, quite different from the other two. This is of an essentially watery landscape, rather dreamlike and insubstantial and is the result of the continuous chain of fresh-water lochs which lie between road and machair, so close together that the villages which are built on the narrow bands of land between them appear to be floating upon the water. Sky, sea, land and lochs have a tendency to merge into a single substance especially on rare hot days when the sky is mirrored in all the watery surfaces so that everything appears to be contained in a large blue bubble, and the quality of the light comes from the evaporation of great quantities of surface water. On the days when the process is reversed and the same water is precipitating in a grey endless curtain, it can seem that the only solid land is the macadamised ribbon unfolding in front of the windscreen wipers.

When I'm on South Uist I nearly always make my base at a thatched cottage, one of four owned by the Gatliffe Trust, which provides primitive accommodation for impecunious island wanderers. Any roof is welcome after camping in the sort of wet windy weather that had followed the Bay Hartavagh idyll, which only goes to show that standards are by no means absolute but are very much conditioned by what has gone before. Just being able to prepare a meal, not lying on my stomach in a cramped space with each movement carefully thought out beforehand so as not to set the tent on fire or spill food all over the interior was a conscious pleasure. A bunk bed with a mattress and a real pillow was also a luxury that compensated a little for the horrid weather; but what I really relished above all other sybaritic, indoor delights was the use of a table and chair. As a sleeping place and a shelter from quite extreme conditions, my tent is a model of what a mere three pounds of nylon can supply, but to attempt to live in a space that does not offer even sitting headroom becomes very trying, especially for those no longer quite as supple as in their youth.

Several other people were also staying at the Howmore hostel, in fact it was fuller than I had ever known it. This was due to the presence on the island of two rare birds which people known as 'twitchers' came from far and wide in order to 'spot' and having spotted to enter on a graded list which rose from mere entries to mega stars.

Stellers eider had been the original attraction but that had been faithfully present for years and everyone who wanted to had already 'bagged' it and it was now thought to have perished of old age. The two new attractions both rated mega stars, one was the pied-billed grebe and the other was the once plentiful corncrake and I had already heard locals muttering that if they could get hold of either bird they would wring its neck as they were sick and tired of 'loonies' trampling through their hay crops in search of them. I was very much on their side having a few days previously been quite shocked when thinking myself to be quite alone on the machair, I had noticed a large cardboard box in the middle of a field. While I was idly wondering what it could possibly be doing there, it had suddenly got up and walked. After the initial shock, I thought I must have been mistaken and that the wind had blown it, but then up it got again and unmistakeably crept a few more stealthy paces forward and even knowing that there must be a person attached to the boots I glimpsed protruding from underneath the box, it still seemed most unnatural and not a little sinister. I feel it gave me some insight into what Macbeth must have felt on seeing a forest marching toward his castle walls.

It was my first encounter with 'twitchers' as opposed to bird watchers and I do not know if they were typical, though to judge from the messages left pinned to the hostel wall, I think perhaps they were. The following is an example of their strange communications:

'Cleaned up on Pied Billed. Got Corncrake on 15th May at Hartlepool bowling green so unless another long stayer rarity turns up on this God-forsaken, windy, wet and unpleasant place I will not have to come back again (unblocked Steller in '83). Is it ever sunny and calm here?'

I didn't think any bird watcher I have known would relate to their subject in quite this way. The difference between the two camps as I see it is that bird watchers have a passion for everything about birds. They spend long periods, often in great discomfort, inconspicuously lurking, in order to study their habits and to take photographs. Whereas twitchers also have a passion but their's is of the collector's variety, like train spotting. The most serious of them will I gather, down tools or anything else at a second's notice and dash to the other end of Britain when news of some inconspicuous but rare avian visitor is rumoured, and once they have it on their list, their interest in it is at an end. Their wealth is their list and although some of them seemed to know a lot about their quarry, others knew only how to recognise the ones they were after. They were not comfortable people to share a small cottage with as they were tramping in and out all night in their indefatigable quest for the mega stars. So when the rain stopped, I found a sheltered place for the tent down among the dunes and had the best of both worlds, a cottage to cook and write in, with occasional company and an undisturbed bed beside an ocean gently thundering on to a white shore.

A young American academic called Don followed my lead and pitched his comfortable larger domed tent among the sand dunes, as did a young English woman named Eva with her smaller ridge tent. Both were glad to escape from disturbed nights in the hostel especially when they found how beautiful it was outside. We spent two evenings lying around warmly wrapped in sleeping bags, watching fat rabbits silhouetted against the luminous starry sky while we talked about the islands. Don was on a six-month walking tour and was particularly interested in the evidence of the prehistoric life of the islands. He had seen wheel houses, souterrains and megaliths on South Uist that I didn't even know existed. He said he didn't think he'd exhaust the possibilities if he stayed another six months and the rain didn't bother him at all. He'd met the most marvellous woman on Lewis who knew more about prehistory than his professor back home and if he could get a research grant he was coming back next year. There was absolutely nothing in the States that was anything like these islands, 'They were really something else altogether.'

Eva was also a first time visitor and as enthusiastic in her own way as Don. She worked for the D.H.S.S. in a depressed area of South London and she'd move up here tomorrow for half the pay she said, if there was a job going. For her, it was the sense of space that was so captivating; she'd been to many of the wilder areas of the British Isles but none of them had had this feeling of openness. She had come up here with her boyfriend, planning to return with him at the end of the week to climb on the mainland, but when the week ended, she'd stayed on and let him go climbing by himself. 'I just felt I wanted to stay here and wander about and not do anything in particular. I don't even mind the rain, in fact I like watching it falling,' she told us dreamily as we sipped mugs of hot soup in the semi-darkness.

I enjoy hearing other people enthuse about places and subjects which delight me, it enhances their value and if I'd spent long with

Eva I might even have come to appreciate rain the way she did. As it was, I felt we were seeing all too little of the sun and would have been happier with the state of affairs enjoyed by Don's prehistoric people. He drew a very idyllic picture of the climate in their day when the islands were covered with woodlands of birch, oak and elm and it was altogether drier and warmer and a pleasure for sleeping out. Since sleeping out was much more common in those times, I suppose this was just as well, especially for the hunter-gatherers who were probably the first people to visit the Long Island — strand hoppers who ate the shellfish from the beach and moved on in their primitive boats, as they'd moved on all along the western coasts of Europe and having got here would soon be running out of land. When they did settle and start to put down roots — though this putting down seems much more a putting up, in the shape of huge megaliths and stone circles, barrows and other noticeable, above the ground objects, it was the sun they appeared to worship. Even in very hot countries with too sparse a rainfall, the sun has invariably been worshipped in ancient times, and I'm quite sure people still do so today, even though they don't call it worship. The truth is everything looks better and people feel happier in sunshine than in rain and if the Outer Hebrides have a fault it is that the rain falls upon them all too frequently and the sun shines not nearly enough.

These other two would have none of my criticisms however. Eva pointed out that the unique flora and fauna of the islands and in fact the whole ethos were direct results of a wet temperate climate. Don more phlegmatically but just as factually said that if the islands enjoyed a sunnier climate they would be inundated with holiday makers and quite spoilt; so on both scores the Outer Hebrides would no longer be the place we all three had fallen in love with. On which philosophical note we ended our discussion for the night and took to our separate tents, for talking about the weather seemed to have provoked another shower.

NINE

There are several big cairns of stone on the east and
the vulgar retain the ancient custom of making a religious tour round them on Sundays and Holidays.

Martin Martin

IN SOME WAYS THE OUTER HEBRIDES OF
around three hundred years ago, when Martin Martin was making
his observations has more in common with the present day than
during the worse decades that intervened. The peasantry that Martin writes about is certainly not downtrodden but full of rude health
and well-being, and in spite of his occasional gibes at their 'Papist
religion', he clearly finds much to admire about them. — 'They are
hospitable, well-meaning people, but the misfortune of their education disposes them to uncharitableness, and rigid thoughts about
their Protestant neighbours,' he wrote.

Over what he saw as their dangerous superstitions he showed all
the prejudice and intolerance of his own anti-Catholic education,
which is a pity, for the glimpses he gives of ancient beliefs and customs are fascinating and whet the appetite for more detail. He wrote
of a glen possessed by the spirits of the 'great men' whose ghostly
voices are heard in the air overhead like summer thunder and who
must be placated if madness is not to strike the person venturing
there: of a stone set up where the church at Howmore can first be
seen, at which spot the people bowed and recited the Lord's Prayer:
of festivals and cavalcades on saints days when 'They bake St.
Michael's cake at night, and the family and strangers eat it at supper'.
But of what St. Michael's cake was made or what form the cavalcades took, or what 'words of power' placated the 'great men' we

learn nothing. It's more than likely that many of the practices were left over from Druid times and had been incorporated into Christian worship — probably the 'tour of the stones' was the right-handed procession around an ancient stone circle or megalith in imitation and honour of the sun, and all pagan festivals featured cavalcades and processions. Martin, very much the inheritor of a rigid Presbyterianism which sits uncomfortably with his curiosity and openness, veers constantly between admiring the purity of the speech and fine 'Irish' scholars of South Uist and despising their credulity and bemoaning the fact that they refuse to be enlightened by the newly installed Protestant minister.

Howmore being the centre of the religious life of South Uist since earliest times, with the remains of an ancient Celtic college and chapels facing the hostel, it was natural to muse over such subjects while watching Shamus Peteranna's cows winding homeward of an evening. After he had introduced me to Jill Maclean who was also interested in the local history, I began to learn more of South Uist's Celtic past. Jill was an English woman who had come to South Uist many years ago to do some post-graduate research on soil types and had never finished her paper, having met and married a local crofter. She and her husband Donald lived a fairly typical island life, their two-bedroomed bungalow, neither aggressively modern, nor picturesquely old and thatched like the hostel, was surrounded with the usual assortment of motor vehicles and machinery, some still functioning and others in various stages of ancient, rusty decrepitude. Facing the bungalow across this busy yard with a few hens roosting among the more permanent features was the old thatched house built by Donald's father, now slowly sliding into a formless heap of stones. Donald had a fishing boat over at Loch Skipport and spent most suitable days catching a kind of velvet crab which was exported to Spain. Jill worked at the Met. Office of the army rocket range at the north of the island. Croft work was fitted in around these two jobs and although they had no children and they must both have worked upwards of twelve hours a day, they seemed to have no more than a low average income.

Amongst Jill's chaotic notes were translations of some of the evidence given to the commission that was set up to enquire into islanders grievances, prior to the writing of the Crofting Act of 1886. Desperately sad reading much of it was, a litany of suffering and indignities which generation after generation had undergone, and underlying it all, a longing to return to traditional lands and holdings. Here I came across the only reference I ever found to Bay Hartavagh:

'My lands were at the back of Ben More. I was put out and settled at Bay Hartavagh and little enough I had there. Now I'm on the west side at Pollacher and I have a horse and two cows and I would give them all if I could be back again behind Ben More.'

Like many relative newcomers, Jill was far more eloquent about the wrongs and injustices of the past than was the average islander and I was glad that she was proposing to set up a local history society in association with people in the other islands. It is high time something systematic was done to preserve living history as well as making a start on properly investigating and preserving the hundreds of historic and prehistoric monuments and buildings of the Outer Hebrides.

I was beginning to get really settled into life in South Uist with a circle of friends expanding daily. I'd even taken to dropping into the hotel at Daliburgh of an evening, where I'd join Mr. and Mrs. Moses and other members of the hospital staff in the bar. I could happily have stayed there indefinitely but the summer was advancing rapidly and if I was going to see anything of the rest of the Outer Hebrides this year it was high time I tore myself away. Before I left the easy 'live and let live' Catholic ethos, and moved on to the more militant and Protestant north however, I felt I had to spend just one more night camping out on the east coast. There hadn't been a twenty-four hour period free of rain in over a week, so in the end I tired of waiting for the ideal day and set out late one blustery but sunny afternoon, with Jill prophesying an imminent gale-force wind before nightfall.

I took the lovely Loch Skipport road past Loch Druidibeg nature reserve, the haunt of divers and greylag geese, where wooded islets, duns and ancient cairns enlivened the wild terrain. A small rhododendron plantation which an earlier rich landowner had planted looked amazingly colourful among the muted shades of the peat hags and heather. Then where the road ended by a mouldering pier I struck out with Evans on a rough track around the south side of the sea loch.

It was a stretch of the coast I hadn't walked yet and didn't know what to expect. The track didn't look much used though within half a mile I came across a small roofed cottage, probably someone's holiday home. The owners would have to bring in any heavy supplies by boat as the track was no longer usable. It had been a good road once, suitable for a pony and cart, but now its bridges were down and with all the rain there had been, each burn was quite a feat to struggle over. One was so deep that I needed to remove boots, socks and trousers and the force of the water made me wish I'd kept them on, as it was very painful scraping along the hidden rocks stubbing toes and grazing shins. Poor Evans lost a lot more paint which I felt guilty about until I remembered that the shop had said it was easy to touch up the paintwork of a black bicycle. I walked along barefooted as there didn't seem a lot of point replacing boots only to have to keep taking them off. It was the first time I'd put foot to ground without the elastic bandage on since the accident and the foot felt very strange without its support. It rained a little out of a blue sky and creamy black mud squelched up between my toes as I walked on, high above the sea. I felt ridiculously happy as though I was enjoying an illicit pleasure inappropriate to a middle-aged woman — though there is absolutely no reason — except for convention, why any person of any age at all shouldn't feel happy to be splashing barefooted in the mud wheeling a bicycle, beside a sparkling sea.

I passed a good few ruins before I found the ideal one for the night's camp, a single, isolated grey structure tucked into the shoulder of a headland with a field of wild iris in front of it, where once a family's food had grown. The roofless house was larger than the one at Bay Hartavagh but the walls were not so beautifully constructed and it had possibly been built a little later I thought. Inside, at one end was a concrete trough, probably a make-do sheep dip, put there after the house was abandoned. It hadn't been used for many years and was half full of bottles, lying in rain water in the trough as though waiting to be washed up. Other bottles, dozens of them lay thickly over the turf inside, half-buried some of them and before I could pitch the tent I had to clear them away. I piled them all into the trough, losing count after 142. I wondered if the place could have served as some sort of rustic drinking club; it had a view worthy of something much grander — the terrace of a millionaire's villa or a perch for a mad Archduke's castle, but I suppose a drinking place in the Outer Hebrides is almost as rare.

There was a small burn falling steeply down to the sea from a spot close to the house with ferns and bushes and a wide variety of other plants growing in the shelter of its banks. Marks of ancient husbandry were all around and the remains of a cow byre was butted up against the far wall of the ruin, opposite the fireplace end. When I noticed this detail, the place seemed suddenly a home and the inhabitants somehow tangible. Strange how this always seems to happen at what the church calls 'the sad hour of compline', when the sun is going down and shadows lengthen. The same hour as a hard-working peasantry would be returning home from their various labours. I wondered whether the people who had raised a family here, living nearly always at the edge of disaster — a wet season, crop failure, poor fishing, sickness — had they ever had the freedom from pressing necessity and numbing poverty to forget it all for one moment and be overwhelmed by the sheer beauty of this scene before me? Remembering their songs and the natural poetry of their language, I felt they must have done, and if for no other reason, than before I went to sleep, I saw from the open doorway of the tent, the loveliest memorial to man's need of beauty for its own sake, beyond the demands of sheer necessity — there was an old, old rosebush which I hadn't noticed until that moment, it was growing out of a rockface at the back of a tiny patch of ground beyond the byre, which had once been a garden. It had almost reverted to its wild state, but not quite and was covered thickly with blossoms.

The promised gale swooped in and raged around me all night, flapping the tent walls about in the most alarming manner and with a noise that made sleep impossible, but the tent stayed up and no water found its way in. In the morning after intermittently dozing and dreaming until hunger forced me to surface more fully, I found the wind to be somewhat diminished but rain was still coming over in short, sharp bursts like machine gun fire. I stayed where I was and prepared a bacon roll and coffee, finding satisfaction in the fact that everything came to hand readily without having to scrabble around in pannier bags for elusive items. Such small delights are the backbone of my type of lightweight camping and afford no end of pleasure while they remain a novelty but like any other limitation, they pall quickly if weather conditions confine my horizons for too long to nothing else.

I wrote up my journal and read a little, but by mid-morning I had had enough of inactivity and steeled myself to the exhausting task of getting out of my sleeping bag and into my clothes while lying in a prone position and not touching the tent walls — which last action destroys the waterproof qualities of the fabric. With only inches of latitude in all directions, this is a feat I have never yet accomplished without a certain loss of goodwill towards the tent designer. I emerged finally hot and ruffled to find only a few last raindrops falling out of a sky flooding with blue and excited seagulls and lapwings tearing about haphazardly, like children celebrating their freedom.

The wind was still strong enough to make it a hard ride back to the main road, where Rueval, the Hill of Miracles bears high on its western flank, the thirty-foot statue of Our Lady of the Isles, gazing out towards the missile range and the Atlantic. Above her, at the summit, a glittering and complex radar installation, known as space city makes a sinister contrast. There is now only the strange flat area of the northern tip of South Uist to traverse which is more water than land. An enormous freshwater loch, Loch Bee connects with the sea at Loch Skipport practically cutting off the north-eastern portion of the island. I avoided the minor road through Gerinish and along the machair, marred now by the scatter of ugly military buildings and the firing range and took instead the main road, which is built on a causeway across the centre of Loch Bee. Flocks of swans were thick upon the water, I've never seen so many altogether. Grey fluffy cygnets sailed with the same effortless progress as their stately parents and I wondered if my particular swan family from Barra had joined this vast assembly. I suppose the feeding here must be particularly good at this time of year for them to gather in such numbers. The road crosses a series of smaller lochs and then the land stops altogether and there in front of me was the peerless world of the South Ford.

How to describe this shallow tidal break in the chain of the Long Island is something for which neither words nor camera have ever seemed quite adequate. The problem is that in a world where the sky already seems larger, higher, more intangible than anywhere else, the effect is somehow doubled at this particular point and one feels in a different element altogether. There are two fords and Benbecula is the small land mass, just four miles long, which separates them — its name means the Mountain in the Fords. The north ford is much wider than the south ford but it is the latter which is the more striking in its effect of light and space and colour. Even Martin Martin waxes lyrical over it and describes a disconnected incident he saw which captures something of the feeling of the place.

'As I came from South Uist I perceived about sixty horsemen riding along the sands, directing their course for the east sea; and being between me and the sun they made a great figure on the plain sands.'

It wasn't until this century that the fords were linked by roads constructed on causeways and bridges. Previously the crossing had been a serious undertaking needing the services of a guide, as the firm footing was always shifting its course. I have found it just as perilous crossing on the road, which is mostly single track, with passing places. Lorries piled high with seaweed, tearing along at full throttle to the alginate works would stop for no-one because their cargo was paid for by weight and every second the load was lightening as the water seeped out of the seaweed. Several times I have only just managed to get out of the path of one of these charging monsters by leaping onto the low parapet and dragging the bicycle up with me; ducking at the same time to avoid the overhanging hanks of seaweed swinging out horizontally with each lurch of the lorry and threatening to topple me from the precarious perch.

I had planned to explore Benbecula thoroughly on this occasion, as previously I had only passed through it on the central road. There are several minor roads running east to join the main road and also a coastal road which runs right round the west side, through more army installations and past the airfield at Ballivanish. To the east several minor roads looked as though they might lead to suitable lonely camping spots. My plans were somewhat modified by finding that the food store at the South Uist end of the ford was closed. As I was clean out of provisions I had to abandon my idea of a picnic overlooking the lovely expanse of sand and instead hurried across to the Co-op on the Benbecula side. This too was closed and I asked a lady who was mowing a handkerchief-sized piece of grass outside her house nearby with an electric mower, where I could find a shop that was open. She said nowhere at all, on account of it being a local holiday and even the Naafi at Ballivanish was closed. The seriousness of the situation had hardly had time to sink in before the woman offered to open up her own store to supply my needs. Strange as it seems, twenty yards from the quite substantial Co-op self service was a small wooden shed where exactly the same kinds of groceries could be bought, at rather higher prices. Since she'd been so obliging I didn't feel I could ask how she coped with such strong competition, perhaps she made do on the custom that occurred outside the Co-op hours. She didn't sell any alcohol as I discovered when I asked for a can of beer, but as I was stowing my purchases into the panniers she went into her house and came out with the present of a can of lager, which must have swallowed any profit she'd made on the transaction.

By the time I'd left the shop and taken a few more minutes to blunt the edge of my hunger with some bread and cheese, I found to my surprise that it was already late afternoon and time to look for somewhere to camp. Island life is often like that, one finds several hours have simply vanished without being able to account for them; part of the reason is because there is so little actual darkness at this time of year, that the tendency is to adapt to a different rhythm and relate to tides and sun rather than clocks.

With the wind hardening from the west, I decided to go with it and do my eastward explorations first, in the hope that the wind would have died or gone round by the following morning, when I would explore the other side.

It was a lonely bleak terrain that I went through first, just wind-blasted heath and peat hags. I was making for Peters Port which looked on the map as though it would be an idyllic spot, overlooking a host of little islets and the larger, bird sanctuary island of Wiay. After a mile, solid land almost ceased and the road continued over small bumps of rock in the sea — causeways and bridges joining nothing to nothing. It was simply an access to the port and when I reached it I found just another rotting pier, almost totally decayed. It transpired that the whole project, road and jetty had been an expensive Victorian folly, hardly ever used because the port had such a dangerous access from the sea, through all those rocky islets. There was no shelter anywhere for a tent and I struggled back against the steadily increasing wind until I could turn north and east again across the next peninsula. Evans fairly flew along past occasional lonely crofts and acres of boggy moors where nowhere at all did there seem to be a dry piece of ground to pitch a tent. In no time I was at the end of the road at Loch Uiskevagh, looking over a scatter of small islands to Rossinish where Bonny Prince Charlie disguised as Betty Burke, a six-foot maid servant had set sail with Flora Macdonald for Skye. It was a very exposed coast, with no shelter it seemed from any point of the compass. Where the occasional hollow offered a minimal buffer to what was clearly the promised gale, of which last night's blow had been merely the prelude — the ground was a morass into which my boots sank above the ankles. I decided to abandon all ideas of camping and instead get back to the main road and see if there was a room available at the old inn by the South Ford.

This was easier said than done. The wind had now risen to a force that seemed pure malevolence. I could not even turn my head in its direction to see where I was going, as bent almost horizontally over

Evans, I attempted to push him along against it. It was difficult even to breathe in the unrelenting buffeting; eight miles would take me forever, even if I could sustain the effort, which I doubted. It would be better to try and find shelter as soon as possible, but where? There were no convenient ruins, the few houses that I had seen on the way appeared abandoned. I almost passed one gate, my eyes half closed and streaming with moisture, before I noticed the reek of peat smoke. I struggled up a rough drive towards the low square bungalow and as I drew near, a face appeared at a window and a hand made gestures for me to go around the back, where a door could be opened out of the path of the wind.

Two bachelors in their mid sixties Hamish and Murdo lived there with their ninety-year-old mother, a frail-looking, white-haired old lady half crippled with arthritis. Murdo managed the croft, and Hamish worked for the military establishment at Balli-vanish. Inside the sudden calm which made my ears ring after the screaming of the wind, I started to explain that I was finding the going a little hard, but I was allowed to get no further. Murdo ushered me into a chair beside a glowing Rayburn stove, while Hamish pushed a kettle to the hottest part of the top plate and started to butter a cut loaf. Their mother directed the proceedings from her nook between stove and window, watching every move her sons made and giving orders in a fast flowing spate of Gaelic.

Not until I had swallowed several cups of tea and demolished a plate of sandwiches and biscuits, amid apologies that there was no scones or home baking was I allowed to give any account of myself. This was typical, unquestioning island hospitality; it would have been no different if I had called on a fine sunny day, for if anyone calls, friend or stranger, food and drink is set before them after which you can enjoy 'a crack' with them. It makes no difference what time of day it is or whether the caller has just been enjoying a 'strupak' in another house, no refusal would be acceptable.

When it was established beyond doubt that I could not manage another morsel nor a further cup of tea, curiosity could be satisfied as to why I was on a seldom visited road in Benbecula with something as peculiar as a bicycle.

'You'd not find a Benbecula man out on a bike on a day like today,' said Hamish.

'No, nor on any day at all, it's motors nowadays for all of you,' his mother chaffed, 'though we were glad enough of bicycles when I was a young woman,' she added.

'But not in a wind like this one,' insisted her son, 'it's enough to blow you into the sea today.'

Murdo said nothing, but just smoked his pipe quietly and watched the proceedings turning from speaker to speaker.

'You'll be from England yourself?' said Hamish in tones that suggested this fact carried more than merely geographical information. I admitted that I was, but added as a mitigating factor, that I had a Scottish grandmother who had been responsible for much of my upbringing.

'Ah well,' said Hamish, 'I was thinking you spoke awful plain for an Englishwoman, that'll be your grandmother's doing no doubt.'

His mother flashed him a warning look and said, 'Whist now Hamish don't be teasing the young lady.'

There was no question of my moving on, as Hamish ingenuously phrased it they were quite happy to put up with me. As it happened they had a caravan belonging to a young relative of theirs who lived in Glasgow. It was parked in a sort of trench between two high banks a little way from the house. Hamish took me along to see if I'd like to sleep there for the night, otherwise I was welcome to stay in the house. It was a perfectly adequate caravan and I was grateful for the use of it. Most of the interior however was filled with a drum kit and in such a state of disarray that I was very glad the old lady could not see it or she would have been mortified. Even Hamish had second thoughts and murmured something about 'young people of today' as he gazed around at the dozens of beer mugs crowding every surface, a green mould growing in many of them. It was the peculiar fungus on the walls that interested me more and on closer inspection I discovered that this was instant potato which the young relative and his musical friends had probably thrown at one another when the music wasn't going well and perhaps it did less harm that way than eating it.

I assured Hamish that I would be perfectly happy in the van and as there was a plentiful supply of water from a pipe outside, I set to and washed up the glasses and removed the mouldy potatoes in a glow of virtue, by way of singing for my supper. Afterwards I retired to bed quite worn out. Not that I slept well, for in spite of the huge pieces of concrete and the ropes and wires anchoring the van, it shook and lifted and banged about in a most alarming manner, and the wind kept rising to fresh crescendos, shrieking and howling like a thousand souls in torment. People told me the following day that it had been as strong a wind as they had experienced anytime that year.

Before I left the next morning I went up to the house to say good-bye and the old lady kissed me and said I must come back soon. She held my hand for a long while before she let me go and said something in Gaelic which I took to be a blessing. Outside the air smelt fresh and the morning was very beautiful after the rain. As I struggled along against the wind still blowing strongly from the west I saw a hawk hanging motionless in the streams of the wind with just the tips of its taut wings fluttering to maintain its station, in a sky that was all tattered streamers and trailing banners of cloud.

Once I'd reached the west coast and could follow its northerly swing, I had the wind to help me for it was swinging round more towards the south-west and Evans sped effortlessly on to Ballivanish, passing old duns and the chapels at Nunton, which had once been nunneries, hence the name. These ruins were mentioned by Martin in one of his anti-Catholic passages. He said that a vault had been discovered in one of the chapels which was full of small bones which some folk said were the bones of birds and others the bones of pygmies, but that one Sir Norman Macleod (a good Protestant) said that it was quite plain that they were 'the bones of infants born to the nuns in the days of popery'. Which pronouncement said Martin with some glee, 'caused the natives to shut up the vault again with great zeal'. I did not stop at the ruins because I was so enjoying just bowling along, after the struggles of the previous day. Even the straight lines and ugly regimented buildings of the large military complex at Ballivanish couldn't spoil the delight of the day. The sky was still so busy organising its complicated cloud patterns that it continually drew the eye to its changing, towering forms and dwarfed everything else to insignificance.

I visited the Naafi store (open to non-military as a goodwill gesture) and was overwhelmed by the variety of produce on display, fresh, frozen and tinned. After ten weeks of island shops I wasn't used to this degree of choice and bought so many 'treats' of fresh meat and vegetables that I had difficulty stowing it all in the panniers. The cyclist runs on food as the car runs on petrol and there is a tendency to stockpile one's essential fuel whenever the opportunity arises.

I left Benbecula with the same benevolent wind propelling me effortlessly over the otherworldly beauty of the North Ford and thought that yet again the island of Benbecula had somehow eluded me. Once more, I had simply passed through, leaving so much that was unexplored that I should feel drawn back there again, forgetting the misery of the gale and the sodden shelterless ground and remembering only the kindness of the people, the hawk hovering in the wind and the magnificence of the skies.

TEN

In this Ile thair is infinite number of fresh water lochis.
Dean Munro

They are a very charitable and hospitable people as is
anywhere to be found. There was never an inn here
till of late, and now there is but one which is not at all
frequented for eating but only for drinking; for
the natives by their hospitality render this newly
invented house in a manner useless. . . .

Martin Martin

T HE SOUTH-EASTERN HALF OF NORTH
Uist is far more water than land. The infinite number of small fresh
water lochs remarked on by the Dean are linked by tattered threads
of peaty ground, which small as they are hold further lochans, so
that only a most circuitous wandering among them is possible. At
the nebulous coastline which is determined only by whether the
water is still fresh or salt, the only difference is that the water itself is
now the link around the infinite number of islets and skerries that
extend for several miles between the solid boundaries formed by
the cliffs of North Lee and Ben Hacklet. It is a tortuous, complicated
topography, much loved by trout fishermen, ducks and wading
birds.

In sunlight this watery area glimmers and sparkles like a many-
faceted jewel, but under grey skies all the colour is drained out of it
and it appears a particularly bleak infertile place, the grey of the
Lewisian gneiss and the uniformly brown heath unrelieved by all
that dark water. Some of the lochs have the remains of ancient
bronze age forts, called brochs in the middle of them approached
by artificial causeways, still in place with trip stones to upset the
unwary and warn the ghosts of that ancient race that strangers are
approaching. These places are redolent of their pagan past and have
a faintly sinister air, as does the huge neolithic chambered cairn that
dominates the landscape from its position on Ben Langass — the

only ground that rises above sea-level for miles around. In an environment where wresting a living could never have been an easy task, such great labours as were needed to raise these huge stone monuments suggest a callousness for human life and dignity commensurate with the building of the pyramids. Possibly the labour was freely given as a spontaneous religious response, but it seems more likely that it was exacted under duress — the age-old exploitation of the weak by stronger forces. Every part of North Uist seems to be under the gaze of some huge menhir, just as in later times Norman castles dominated the landscape of England and Wales kept an oppressive watch on the conquered Saxons. The best stone-age monuments of the Outer Hebrides are further north, on the west coast of Lewis, but it is in North Uist that they seem such a conscious presence.

The only village of any size is on the east coast of this watery area, at Loch Maddy. Here the car ferry puts in, threading its way through the plethora of little islands. Once the huge anchorage was a centre for the herring fishery. The fishing had always been good, long before the herring gained such popularity and King Charles I had planned all sorts of schemes for expanding the white fish trade and had even begun some of the building work, before he lost his head, thereby putting an end to the scheme. Cromwell had little interest in the place, apart from sending a few gun boats to subdue the natives, one of which split itself asunder on some rocks further south.

Someone who had enjoyed a success with fish that poor Charles I was not allowed time for is George Jackson, another white settler who felt strongly drawn to the Outer Hebrides and determined to make a life for himself on North Uist. George has a fish shop and to appreciate how rare and exotic this is in these parts, it would be necessary first to try and buy a fresh fish anywhere else in these islands. Some of the shops have packets of fish fingers, I've even seen those cook-in-a-bag, boneless offerings, but good honest, unadulterated fish, straight from the surrounding seas or the lochs goes anywhere except on to local dinner tables. Nor is it often possible to obtain any of the delicious shellfish caught locally, that goes straight away to the Continent or to London. So when I came across the Mermaid Fish Supplies, with a list of produce that included monkfish, fresh scallops, crab claws and all the usual white fish, I could hardly believe my eyes and had to go straight in and ask George what had inspired the project.

Like many people with a true passion, George was only too happy to take a few hours out of his busy day to satisfy my curiosity and during the course of the morning I learnt something of his very interesting life story. His road to the Isles had been a circuitous one which had taken him most of the way around the world before finishing at this small clachan on the west coast of North Uist. As a young, newly-qualified engineer he had accepted a six-months contract, surveying for minerals in the wilder regions of Ecuador. From there he had gone to Canada, to the Hudson River to follow up a relationship which didn't work out, and to take up a position in a power station, which didn't actually exist when he arrived. Robbed and penniless he obtained a job as a welder on an Arctic rocket range doing exploratory work on the Aurora Borealis. With the typical Scottish ability to turn his hand to anything, particularly of a mechanical nature, he redesigned their launching pad, which was not functioning as it should and then set to and put the design into practice — it worked. In 1969 he returned to Scotland, working his passage on a German freighter. He was now 28, well travelled and with a lot of hard-won confidence, but without capital or prospects. He took a temporary job out of necessity and it happened to be at a seaweed processing plant at Loch Maddy, which was being modernised. It was while working there that he saw the croft at Clachan for sale and knew that he had found his niche, the place where he wanted to settle down.

Not that anything was going to be plain sailing, to begin with, an American woman had already decided to buy the croft and it was no easy matter for George to persuade her to relinquish her claim. Somehow he managed this and found himself in possession of an all but ruined cottage surrounded by a small patch of not particularly fertile ground and £750 in the red. He did several jobs including cutting seaweed for the factory, in order to pay his way and stay on the island. At the same time there was the house to re-roof and make habitable. It was too much for one man alone, so he thought up a scheme for offering working holidays to young people, who in return for their food would put in several hours a day fencing, ditching and filling in the gaps in the cottage walls. This worked after a fashion but it did not please some of the locals, who imagined all sorts of iniquities resulting from young people of mixed sexes cohabiting and strong representation was made to him, to the effect that it would have to stop.

In the meantime George had hit upon the idea of supplying fish to the islanders as a means of achieving an independent life style. At first he caught the fish himself, going out in a small boat with a net and selling his catch from door to door the following day; doing his rounds by scooter with a fish box on the back. He was surprised that several local people took exception to being sold yesterday's catch, especially as even Billingsgate can't turn fish around quicker than that. The idea of a shop was the turning point; he built it in 1976 and so far it has gone from strength to strength. The various grants, especially the Integrated Development Programme were tailor-made for someone like George and he had made the most of them. He now has a large cold room (this was obtained from the Naafi who were getting rid of it) a vacuum packaging machine, bread crumber, fish smoker, weighing machines etc. He employs two other people fulltime and also part-time help, working long hours himself and thriving on it. Fishermen are prepared to sell him their catch because they know he will take anything as long as the quality is good and that he will be prepared to drive anywhere on the islands at any time to collect it, which is more convenient for the fisherman than sending the catch to Oban.

Like many people who demand a great deal from themselves, he is not prepared to accept less than professional standards from others, which is not easy for islanders to adapt to after centuries of a quite different approach to life and I gather that his Saturday boy is surprised to be told that he may not arrive an hour late for work when something else has turned up for him to do. George has a running battle with the engineer in charge of island roads too, for the huge bumps and potholes which can go unattended for months or even years can exact an expensive toll on George's transport, hurrying to pick up a catch from a fishing boat waiting to sail on the tide.

Apart from direct grants George's main concern has been to obtain expertise in the practical aspects of the fishmongers art. He has found some difficulty in this, as experts employed by the Board have often seemed happier handing out theoretical advice rather than rolling up their sleeves and demonstrating how, for example, to slit a whiting in preparation to turning it into an Arbroath smokie. By tenaciously insisting on what he wants he has eventually acquired the various techniques to the point where his salmon, smoked to his own unique recipe is sent all over the world and I can certainly vouch for its excellence, it was at least as good as any I'd ever had anywhere. He is also beginning to supply the fast growing chain of co-operatives with vacuum packed real fish, but he still sees his main market as being on North Uist itself and has no intention of expanding into a large concern; as it is, he thinks he has got it just right.

No-one I feel could dispute the fact that George has earned his success, battling with such energy and perseverance against island apathy and entrenched attitudes. I wouldn't want his job — hard, finger-chilling work that it is, but I could with great contentment live in the lovely home he has made out of the leaky old croft house. It is rather small but it enjoys tremendous views over the huge, almost land-locked sands of Oithir Mor towards the Balranald Bird Sanctuary and the open sea. The interior is a triumph of ingenuity, combining the basic lines of an old croft house with enough modern amenities to make for comfort as well as great attractiveness. He shares it now with a wife whom (typical of his whole approach to life) he took great trouble to acquire. Since he wasn't encouraged to continue his working parties, where he might well have found a like-minded partner, and since he couldn't leave his business to go in search of the right woman, he sought the aid of an agency which deals in such matters. The result I was assured by many people has been a great success and as they both love their island life and one another and have an occupation that is unlikely to suddenly fail. I count George as being among the most contented of people whom I met on the Outer Hebrides.

It is on the west coast, a little to the south of Geroge Jackson's place that I like to stay on North Uist, at another of the Gatliffe Trust hostels. This one would be just another mouldering ruin replaced like so many others of its kind with unattractive modern bungalows built with E.E.C. grants, were it not for the Trust whose concern is as much to preserve these old houses as to provide accommodation. Island people are no longer prepared to live in three-roomed houses, with little or nothing in the way of 20th Century improvements, but it is a pity that these unique dwellings are so little valued that they are allowed to rot, for they enhance the landscape, whereas what replaces them can hardly be said to do that. More imaginative and enlightened spending could surely turn them into something as desirable and attractive as George's croft, at a fraction of the cost of the new kit-bungalows and whereas they would be too small for a family, the average age of islanders is well over sixty and so there are plenty of older couples which they could suit very well.

The hostel sits in the middle of fields, on a low green knoll, looking like something that grew there naturally, a comfortable, dumpy shape, topped by thick thatch with a border of stones suspended from the edges of the herring net which holds it down against the gales. A green path meanders across the fields towards it. Hens scratch about in front of the door and a rooster takes his stand on the peatstack to wake the hostellers each morning. The chemical loo is in a shed that doubles as a calfhouse in the winter, and water is obtained with a bucket from the standpipe in the yard. Rooster, hens and calves belong to Mrs. Tosh, who was born there and whose father first built the house. She and her husband and family live in a new bungalow by the roadside, called 'Seabreeze', on the other side of the field and cater for B&Bs. She leads a very busy life with the family, croftwork and the B&Bs, but although the hostel has added to her load she says she loves to see it there whenever she raises her eyes from what she is doing, all refurbished and with the new thatched roof just as it was in her childhood. The rethatching had been carried out the previous winter by Mrs. Tosh herself, for there are few people left who know how to do it. Fortunately her father had taught her the skill and since Hebridean thatch lasts only about three years, it's to be hoped that Mrs. Tosh will be able to pass on her knowledge to someone else.

There is room for only eight people at a time at Cladach and even this number is quite a squeeze for the two and a half small rooms, so a good deal of co-operation is needed for even the shortest stay and it couldn't really be described as comfortable. It does have charm however and the Toshs are assembling a wealth of old farm implements and machinery around the place, which adds to the atmosphere of being in the middle of crofting life of earlier times and so visitors are prepared to put up with the discomfort. There were several couples already installed, French, German and American, the three Glasgow twitchers and Eva, who had camped beside me on South Uist. Eva and I shared the half room which had two sleeping shelves built into it, one above the other, the top one so near the ceiling, that the sleeper (me as it happened) seemed to have invaded the moth and spider realm. It was necessary to go to bed one at a time, so limited was the space. Some of the others slept outside in tents so there were more than eight present and even preparing meals in shifts, it was not easy to manage. Fortunately the twitchers moved on after one night and since they were the least organised and had the most equipment this made a big difference to everyone else's comfort.

This part of North Uist has a much gentler aspect than the eastern side because of all the sand and the machair, and yet it is in a con-stant state of change and tragedy as the sea continues inexorably to claim the land — a piece here and another there, widening channels and making peninsulas into islands; and in the past destroying town-ships and communities. The Monach Isles once inhabited and accessible at low tide are now totally cut off, eight miles out to sea. I spent several days ambling about the area on Evans, and wherever I went meant hard going at some point in the day, for on this low lying land there is little to break the force of the wind, and it blew inces-santly throughout my stay. It was cold for the time of year, but bright and more like early spring than full summer. Showers came over at frequent intervals but they were so short-lived that it wasn't worth donning rain gear, especially in the wind, as it flapped about acting as a sail, threatening to unseat me. If I miscalculated the dura-tion of a squall and got unpleasantly wet, it was never long before the wind dried me out again.

It was wonderfully exhilarating to be on high ground in this sort of weather, and as my ankle continued to improve I found I could ride the rougher hill paths and the ridges of the trackless moors. From there the whole island spread out like a map below — the scat-ter of glittering lochans to the south and east, while to the west were colours never matched in any jewellers shop, as the water passing over the sands changed depth and shaded down from palest jade to deep cobalt blue. I'd make sure I was on one of the low hills near the coast, like Crogary Mor or Sgur an Dun for my lunch stop so as to enjoy the prospect while I cooked up soup or something else warm-ing on my stove. I was always so hungry in that fresh sea air that I found it necessary to carry plenty of provisions around; treats like George's crab claws were delicious eaten with plenty of bread and butter and with a steaming mug of tea to warm my hands on.

Although a bicycle is a wonderfully quiet means of transport, enabling its rider to take in an endless stream of observations through most of the senses, it's often not until I've actually stopped and sat quietly for a while that a full awareness of the surroundings really floods over me. I might have been thinking how lovely this or that particular thing is, but my mind has probably been preoccupied with other matters and when I sit there it is as though I'm seeing it all for the first time. There was one day like that on North Uist which I particularly remember. I'd ridden up a track to the summit of Beinn Riabach, a small hill on the north-west extremity of the island. It was one of the most beautiful and impressive views I had ever seen.

The sky was full of pillars of cloud, changing their shape constantly before the strong westerly wind and the jade colours of the sea were flecked with white where the wind whipped up the crests. It was low tide so that great areas of Vallay Strand and the sands beyond were exposed and the shadows of the racing clouds with patches of blue sky in between were reflected on the wet surfaces. Beyond the shallows the water was a dark bluish purple, banded with white and a deep white fringe edged the three off-shore islands of Boreray and Berneray and the taller Pabbay behind, where great waves which had gathered their force across two thousand miles of ocean were dashing themselves against the cliffs. To the West on the headland at Kilphedder the beautiful ancient granite cross found in a burial ground and set up now on a high plinth stood like a sentinel against the sea.

I moved on to the Youth Hostel at Loch Maddy for my last Saturday on North Uist as I felt in need of less rudimentary washing facilities than the standpipe at the Clachan hostel afforded. The inclement weather had put me off bathing in the sea or in a loch, especially knowing that hot water was available at no greater cost than submitting to Youth Hostel rules. Actually the warden at Loch Maddy runs a pleasant hostel and is very relaxed except about bedtime, which is really all to the good and I found it quite helpful to be chased away to bed at eleven p.m. for once, rather than to remain chatting with other hostellers until the small hours. My stay there stretched to three nights as I couldn't leave on Sunday there being no ferries on the Sabbath and on Monday I found I had run out of methylated spirits for my stove and so had to go on a tour of the island to try and find some. I had hopes that the shop at Loch Maddy, the WEEHAVIT might live up to its name but although they were triumphant about replacing my lost lipsalve, meths were beyond them and they suggested that I try the hotel. I realised afterwards that they must have thought that it being a spirit it would be found behind a bar. Not long ago meths was a necessity in these parts for priming Tilley lamps, the main source of lighting, but now nearly everywhere has electricity and as there are obviously no meths drinkers in the country that invented whisky, the commodity has become very rare. It took me the whole of Monday to track down the only source of supply, which was in a remote clachan right down at the south end near the ford, where eventually, after locating the old man who kept the store I came away triumphantly clutching two half whisky bottles filled with the mauve liquid.

I didn't mind the diversion because it gave me a chance to see again the interesting ruins of the medieval monastery of Teampul na Trionaid — Church of the Trinity, destroyed in the Reformation but once the place where the sons of the nobility were educated. Substantial ruins are so rare in these parts that where they occur they assume a heightened significance; these lichened remains with their finely arched window recesses look suitably melancholy against the empty rough landscape.

It was very noticeable how kind people had been to me on this Monday, I'd been offered innumerable cups of tea as I'd made my enquiries and on several occasions when I'd been looking at my map, people had stopped their cars to ask me if I was lost and to offer help. This was in marked contrast to the mood of the previous day when I'd been only too aware that I had passed the invisible line that divided the Catholic south from the Presbyterian north and was now in an area where the Sabbath was treated with the utmost seriousness. I'd hardly seen anyone about, only a few cars full of black clad people on their way to kirk. No-one had smiled or waved to me, as they would on any week day and when I'd arrived at the end of a lonely road, which had wound through the strings of lochs and peat cuttings of Loch Portain, I'd had dogs set on me. At first I'd thought it was coincidence that a door had opened and a couple of growling collies had been ejected by an unseen hand just as I was passing a house. I was on a rough track though not a private one, which led to a headland where I'd planned to make a stop and look at the dun on the small island opposite. The dogs came straight at me, hackles raised and teeth bared but fortunately they responded to my 'Lie down' and 'Go home' uttered with more confidence than I felt. I saw a curtain twitch in the window behind them and knew I was being watched. When I came back an hour or so later a man of about sixty stood on the step and deliberately turned his back as I called a greeting. In spite of having met other displays of this type of Sabbatarianism before in many different parts of the Highlands and Islands I find it difficult not to feel disturbed by it.

When I reached the road a shower started and I was invited to shelter in a camper van which was parked there. It was owned by a Belgian couple with two children who had been spending a couple of months each summer on the Outer Hebrides for the last four years. They had had the dogs set on them too, but were not unduly bothered. 'Ah crazy people,' they said. 'They think it's holy to set the dogs on people just because they are walking. We should all be miserable because it's Sunday?' We drank delicious coffee, such as I hadn't had since leaving London and talked about why we came back to the islands again and again, in spite of weather, dogs and Sabbatarianism, while the children scampered in and out between showers. Marie Ann, the wife had no doubts about what drew her. It had to do she said, with the sense of space out here, a quality that she was sure had a spiritual dimension. It was something that was a necessity, something you had to keep coming back to having discovered it, because modern city life was so devoid of it. Her husband Frank said he saw it more as freedom from pressure and conformity, and he said the children became totally different when they were here, much calmer and less demanding. Marie Ann who was doing a degree course was spending this holiday writing up her thesis, quite a feat I though in a small camper van with the family under foot. She said it was easier than being at home, as the children amused themselves and whenever she needed a break she had only to lift her head and look out of the window.

They both harboured dreams about living out there permanently, and like me, they looked speculatively at every empty house. They had never seen anything that was quite ideal, since nearly all island houses are built facing the road, their windowless backs turned resolutely to any view. This was really a relief to Marie Ann and Frank as they would have hated to have found the ideal place, knowing that there was no way they could make a living there as foreigners. The foreigners who did buy property in the islands — mainly Swiss, German and Dutch were usually extremely wealthy and wouldn't need to worry about windows, for whatever they bought, they could probably afford to turn the whole thing around.

*   *   *

Continuing my journey northwards was a much simpler process by bicycle. A motorised traveller wanting to proceed northwards up the Long Island goes next to Harris and to do this must take the MacBraynes steamer from Loch Maddy and sail back to Skye and from there to Tarbert, in the north of Harris, a long detour, taking a whole day or even two days if boats don't connect. The cyclist on the other hand has only to cycle a few miles along a pleasant winding road, past innumerable Stone Age monuments, to Newtonferry, just a short bowshot from the small island of Berneray. From here a local ferry takes less than an hour to reach Leverburgh in the south of Harris. To my surprise, after I had ridden the last delightful mile, which switchbacks up and down miniature cliffs besides a shallow translucent sea, I found there were now two separate boats. Previously a half-decked little vessel, with a tall narrow wheelhouse sticking up like a chimney from the deck had made the rolling pitching crossing, calling first at its home port of tiny Berneray, where only I and a local or two and the district nurse making her rounds had alighted. On very calm days I'd seen this tippy little boat transporting motor vehicles tied to two planks amidships and protruding several feet on either side; it had looked extremely perilous.

All that was changed now; the small half-decked boat was replaced by a smart fibreglass launch with carpet in the saloon, where the pilot, no longer jams himself into the isolation of his wheelhouse but sits among the passengers on a swivel chair in front of an impressive consul. Radar and echo sounders now add their modern aid to the boatman's age-old inherited knowledge of the tortuous channels through the maze of islands and rocks in the Sound of Harris. Even more revolutionary is the recently installed car ferry which plies across the couple of hundred yards of shallow water that separates Berneray from North Uist. Berneray is three miles long and a mile and a half wide and has at most six miles of roads. The islanders would have liked a bridge or a causeway to link them to a wider world, but even a car ferry for the use of just 150 people is quite a revolution.

ELEVEN

Beside this lyis ane Ile callit Berneray als lang, als braid als plentifull.

Dean Munro

This island in the summer is covered all over with clover and daisy, except in the cornfields.

Martin Martin

Tʜᴇ ꜱᴏᴜɴᴅ ᴏꜰ ʜᴀʀʀɪꜱ ᴡʜɪᴄʜ separates Harris from North Uist is the largest gap in the Long Island chain. A considerable population once lived on the innumerable small islands which over the millennia have become separated from the main land mass and now lie scattered in profusion over the wide expanse of sea. Of the three larger islands — none of them more than about three square miles in extent — only Berneray has remained in continuous occupation. Pabbay its nearest neighbour once supported more than 300 souls, before it was cleared in the 19th century for sheep. The inhabitants of Boreray, a little further off, held out until 1923 when they requested evacuation to somewhere less remote. One family surprisingly, at the last moment elected to remain and work the whole island and it continued to be farmed by a single family until quite recently. This however was very unusual; the difference between life on a small off-shore island being tenable for a community or not hangs on a hairsbreadth and with the changing standards and expectations of the 20th century all of them except Berneray have been abandoned, mainly because of the difficulty of maintaining communication during the winter months, when continuous gales can rage for weeks on end. Berneray is therefore especially precious as the last inhabited island of the Sound of Harris and it is to be hoped that the provision of the car ferry will halt further erosion of the dwindling population.

At the last count there were a hundred and forty-eight inhabitants of Berneray and one single hippie, named Chris. I am never really sure what a hippie is supposed to be and have myself been so called by Tibetan children trying to sell me 'magic mushrooms' in the Kulu Valley. I think that perhaps anyone who is doing something different from the norm is in danger of being given this title. The people of Berneray seem rather proud of their 'hippie' and indeed they have no reason not to be. I only met him by accident, drawn through insatiable curiosity to an unusual oriel window, high in the gable end of a tiny building which was so close to the edge of the sea that I should have thought there was a great danger of it being washed away in a high tide. Seeing me negotiating Evans over the slippery rocks, Chris who tends to be somewhat wary of people, must have decided that I did not constitute a threat, for he came to the door and when I had expressed my admiration for his house, he asked me in for a cup of home-made soup and a closer look round.

Following the practice of placing people into convenient slots Chris would be labelled a drop-out artist. Like many sensitive people he had had some sort of emotional crisis. It had happened towards the end of his art course and as a result of it he found he could no longer cope with the life he had been living and had to get right away. He was fortunate in that he had a friend who had already discovered Berneray and he came to live with him and began to explore different values such as Buddhism, and to live a self-sufficient existence, fishing and growing vegetables, crossing over to North Uist to cut peat and so forth. Chris thinks that this sort of island life prevented him having a total nervous breakdown. After a while it became necessary for him to have his own place to live — 'his own space' as he called it, and this degree of independence which was really forced upon him by his friend, turned out to be crucial, for the friend upon whom he had so depended was drowned shortly afterwards in a canoeing accident, a loss which might well have destroyed Chris's new found fragile balance.

Property on Berneray is scarce and the only place Chris could find was the ruin of an old abandoned cattle byre in close proximity to someone's croft. The owner let him have the place together with a tiny patch of ground alongside for growing vegetables and Chris set to and slowly built himself a home of such charm, character and ingenuity that I found it difficult not to envy him it. Into its building has gone all the creativity which Chris hadn't felt able to put onto canvas. He says he has grown strong in the process and I think the house reflects something of his inner struggles. It can't have been an easy task, even on the simplest level; as I've mentioned elsewhere, any building work on the Outer Hebrides is a triumph of perseverance and flexibility. When you haven't any money either and have to do your contriving out of what other people have discarded, it must at least double the difficulties. In Chris's case fighting at the same time not to be overwhelmed by the dark forces threatening to destroy him, I think the outcome has been a most tremendous triumph. If he were my son I would be very proud of him and happy that he had found this degree of peace and fulfilment on a beautiful island among an accepting and supportive community.

He isn't out of the woods yet though and even on Berneray he still finds times of great difficulty. I was there during the newly instituted Berneray week when attempts are made to provide group entertainment and activities, especially for expatriates back for a holiday. There was a ceilidh one night, held in the dilapidated hall and I went along to it with Chris. We sat on hard backless benches, packed closely together and it was clear from the outset that Chris was finding the occasion extremely difficult. He was in a state of obvious tension, beads of moisture standing out on his forehead, his knuckles white with gripping the edge of the bench. It was only with seemingly great difficulty that he was able to remain there until the first interval, when he made his excuses and fled.

Perhaps one day he will be able to find his way again as an artist. I certainly hope he does, for although I saw very little of his work, just a poster and a couple of pencil sketches, these showed all the talent and the surprising wit and humour that is apparent in the construction of his small house. He had other plans for his immediate future; the next day he was leaving the island to spend a few weeks working with a theatre group, designing sets for them and painting scenery. He had met them the previous year when they had been touring the islands with a mime and puppet show. Chris said that he had found their work so exciting that he had just gone off with them there and then, for the rest of their summer tour. They had since acquired permanent premises in a northern town and had invited him down on a professional basis to work with them, which clearly meant a great deal to him.

It was strange that I hadn't met Chris before or noticed his house because I had stayed several times on Berneray and had, I thought, explored it thoroughly, which just goes to show that even on the smallest of islands it is always possible to find something new. The reason I mostly stopped off here, apart from the great attractiveness of the island itself was the existence of the third of the Gatliffe Trust hostels, which is situated in the most idyllic of positions, even to the extent of facing in the right direction, looking out over the Sound of Harris. I had spent so long looking at the view from the windows of that cottage that it had become a place I dreamed about whenever I felt overwhelmed by one of the concrete wastelands which are springing up everywhere in rapidly 'modernising' countries like Syria, Jordan or Libya, where the combination of heat, dust, noise, smell and inhuman architecture (perpetually unfinished) combine to make the traveller yearn for remote green places, entirely surrounded by water — I think it was no accident that the psalms with their emphasis on 'green pastures' and 'still waters' were written in the Middle East — and that was even before concrete had been invented.

The Ordnance Survey map shows the small thatched cottage, which is the hostel, as being practically in the sea and indeed at high water on a spring tide seals will sometimes swim close enough to the windows for the delighted watcher to be able to gaze straight into their so very human, brown eyes while sitting inside the hostel having a meal. I've taken out a recorder and played them tunes at such times, not daring to inflict my singing upon them, and as long as I've kept up the recital they've stayed there, flatteringly attentive. These are the great grey Atlantic seals, Ron Mor, the Selkie of the old legends — 'I am a man upon the land, I am a selkie in the sea. And when I'm frae from the land, my dwelling is in the Sule Skerrie.' They were supposed to have both a human and a sea nature and to be the bridge by which man could cross the gulf that he had created between himself and the animal kingdom. Mermaids seem to be a much later invention, developed from the Selkie legends. Nearly all the old stories about seals coming into contact with the human world are sad and emphasise the inability of man to allow other creatures to be themselves without wanting to change them. The archetypal ones are where a man comes upon a young seal in her human form and falls in love with her. She lives with him and bears his children and all seems well until one day the sea calls her. Torn though she is by love for the man and for her human children, the pull of the wilder life of the ocean and of the seal people is ultimately too strong to resist. Ever afterwards he haunts the tideline seeking his Selkie wife and at the turn of the tide, she sometimes keeps a vigil from a far skerrie where she can see the light in his cottage window.

Another seal story that haunted me ever since I heard it is about direct exploitation. A lonely old woman finds a young seal on the beach and persuades it to come back to her cottage for a while to tell her the secrets of the sea. Afterwards she cannot bear to lose the lovely creature's company and keeps it prisoner, only letting it go into the sea each day to fish at the end of a long rope, but the young seal cannot live in captivity and daily grows weaker and ever closer to death. Then one day while it is swimming in the sea, the old woman holding tightly to the end of the rope, the seal's mate swims into the bay. He has sought for her through the length and breadth of the world's oceans and now he urges her to swim out with him to the open sea. Desperately the young seal strains against the rope, trying to follow her lover and just as desperately the old woman hauls on her end of it, until eventually the rope grows slack in her hands and she hauls in the young seal, quite dead, her heart having burst with the effort to win freedom.

Seals breed now on some of the islands in the Sound, which they would not have done in earlier times when they were killed for food and for oil for the lamps. They are occasionally shot at by fishermen who regard them as something of a menace, both because of the fish they eat and the damage they can do to their nets. They are not hunted systematically however and their worst enemy is the killer whale who seem to feed on them in preference to any other food. So in many respects Ron Mor has a happier life than some other species of fur seal, and currently their numbers are increasing.

The deep water channel, just a foot or so wider than the ferry boat runs about eighty feet in front of the hostel and at low tide the water falls to the edge of this channel, exposing a large area of winkle covered boulders; the rest is sand. Once I saw an otter here with two cubs at heel, frolicking along among the rocks and under the long fronds of seaweed, another immensely exciting and all too rare a sight. Seals and otters both have a special quality that moves the heart, foxes have it too, to some extent. I think the nub of their appeal is that they seem to find a joy and interest in life over and above food seeking and mere survival. It is impossible not be anthropomorphic about them because they play as human children do, spontaneously, and with apparent delight.

When I first came here, about ten years before, there was one other house occupied in this ancient little settlement of about seven dwellings on the sea's edge. The other five were in the process of collapsing in upon themselves, without squalor as everything domestic had been removed from them. Their few remaining timbers were already bleached as white as bone and the stones were gradually being covered by the fine sand: they had almost returned to the fabric of the island. There were no gardens around the houses; there might have been some once, but now there was no trace of them. The houses rose out of the green, sandy turf without foundations or fences, other than the odd strand of wire, intended to keep off the sheep and failing miserably (in compensation the wire served excellently for hanging out wet clothes). Just as in Martin Martin's time, clover and daisies were thick upon the ground everywhere, also buttercups, scabious, eyebright, selfheal, speedwell, sheepsbit and a host of other close growing little plants. The other occupied house was in its original state and as pretty as a picture under its thick thatch, with whitewashed walls and red geraniums in the deep embrasures of the tiny windows. An old lady had lived there alone, her three rooms as neat and clean as a new pin, even the copper piping of the stove was polished. She had sometimes asked me in for a cup of tea and I remember her sitting there knitting an endless succession of huge white Aran sweaters, for sale in mainland shops; she also looked after the hostel. Then her sister had died over in Skye leaving her a house there, and she had left the island. How she made this choice I never learnt, though I have an idea that she was not a native of Berneray and had been rather lonely there after all her near neighbours had departed.

The hostel is now looked after by the sixty-year-old unmarried twin sisters, Jessie and Annie, who live together on their farm half a mile away. Berneray is famous for its twins, each generation having produced a greater number of them than anywhere else on record. The Macleod twins are such exact replicas of one another — plump, white-haired ladies, with beautiful complexions and shy smiles — that I cannot tell them apart, even when they are standing side by side; the effect, particularly of the identical smiles is distinctly uncanny. In all the conversations I have had with them they never once said 'I', even if it was one twin on her own; whatever point of view or information was being given it was always by 'We'. This can seem rather grand and royal if the existence of the other twin isn't known about — which was the case when I first met them. I became thoroughly confused too especially when referring to the subject of a conversation I'd been having with one of them the previous day only to be met by blank incomprehension, so that I'd wonder if my memory was playing me tricks. From the number of times this happened before one of them said, 'Oh it will have been my sister you were talking to, we are very alike,' I rather suspect that the twins derive a certain amount of entertainment from the confusion. Berneray people have no such problems of course since they've known the twins from birth and it's all a matter of familiarity — even sheep which look identical to everyone else can be identified immediately by their shepherd.

The twins own several Berneray houses and have recently added to them the old lady's abandoned cottage by the hostel, so I suppose they are by way of becoming local property tycoons. However they don't seem to want to make money out of their property and I wouldn't be surprised if they'd only acquired it for sentimental reasons. There is a quality about these two ladies which reminds me of the seals and otters. They have somehow retained a childlike delight in things which most of us lose with age, to our disadvantage.

'We are very fond of animals,' is the most frequent remark that crops up in their conversations and I have the distinct impression that they really prefer animals to people. They treat their cats and dogs as pets, which is rare in the islands where most people regard these animals as purely for work and keep them outside. Even so the twins' dogs are models of obedience and this in spite of the fact that I've never heard either twin issue a command to them above the level of a gentle murmur, yet even the young dog, Roy which they had with them this year flattened himself to the ground in abject shame and contrition when given the gentlest of rebukes. They keep hens, sheep and several cows for raising beef, but they say that the work is getting too much for them and that they will give up the cattle soon. This will I'm sure be a wrench for them. I see them sometimes going across the fields with buckets of milk for the sucking calves which spend their days tethered away from the house and it's plain that it's a pleasurable activity, rather than a chore, from the way they stay and pet the animal long after it's finished the milk.

In spite of complaining about having much to do, Jessie and Annie 'relax' by spending hours gathering sacks of winkles from the rocks in front of the hostel.

'Oh we just love the winkling and it's so healthy out here by the sea,' they told me when I asked them what they were doing. They showed me their buckets half filled in a surprisingly short time, a small eel and an even smaller flounder had been added to their spoils 'For the cat'. To my regret they were wary of my camera, suspecting me of wanting to take what they considered were unsuitable pictures of them. I had been charmed by the shapes they made and the contrast with the sharp edged rocks as they bent over their task and was about to take what I considered a rather Manet type photograph when they noticed what I was doing and immediately stood upright, fixing me with the disapproving look they reserved for Roy at his most disobedient. The last thing I wanted was to upset them so I went over to explain what it was I was trying to do, but I didn't manage to allay their suspicions.

'It was our bottoms you were taking, you rogue,' they chided me, only half in jest I thought. 'We were in a picture right enough with Prince Charles and Diana,' they said proudly, 'but we had our best clothes on then.' That I wanted to take them as they were in their everyday wrap over aprons and gumboots had displeased them as much as what they thought was the unsuitable pose.

It seemed that everybody in the Long Island had harboured ambitions of appearing in the local paper during the royal visit, all of course in their best clothes, and in as close proximity to the royal pair as possible. The tour had been planned so that all the islanders would have the opportunity of seeing 'the Royals' and the local newspaper photographers had worked hard to feature as many local faces as possible — very wise of them as it must have enhanced the paper's sales greatly. Whether several special editions had been published I'm not sure but on every island I was shown page after page of closely packed photographs of the occasion and to be included there carried the same prestige as appearing on the society pages of the Tatler. I gather that all the 'Twins of Berneray' had been assembled to meet the royal pair and have their photograph taken and after such a prestigious experience I had even less chance to take the sort of pictures I wanted.

Although the hostel is so idyllically placed it was not idyllic in itself, being so damp and decayed that only one room was really habitable and then only after a fire had dried it out somewhat, but it made a good base and outside, the enormously deep window embrasures provided comfortable sun traps in which to sit sheltered from the wind while gazing across the Sound to the grey hills of Harris and all the myriad of small islets in between. It is the sort of scene that never palls for there is always so much activity going on in it; if it isn't inquisitive seals or the rare otter, then strings of shag or cormorants are preening their feathers on the rocks before they plunge into the sea, appearing again far away, having pursued their prey with swift and deadly effect beneath the waves. Their successes can be clearly seen from the way they surface, swallowing hard. The sudden plummeting fall of a gannet diving on the fish arrests the attention always, with a start like a missed heart beat and each time I have to keep watching in case I shall see one emerge bearing a fish speared through upon its beak. They do take fish this way and there is a tale, that if St. Kildans found one of their number had committed a murder, not being prepared to execute him themselves, they would tie him to a board and float him out on the sea with a fish fastened to his throat and let the gannets despatch him. It seems that St. Kildans also caught gannets by placing fish on planks, when the hapless birds would pierce right through the wood with the force of their dive. They apparently have extraordinary binocular vision which is what enables them to spot their prey from such tremendous heights. No bird, not even the osprey, makes quite such a spectacle as he fishes; it is the dazzling whiteness falling like a bright comet that is the wonder of the bird. In contrast, the clowns of the tideline, the oyster catchers provide a totally different and quite delightful spectacle. Plump, black and white little birds, they look like very small harlequins who are wearing very long, false red noses and Venetian face-masks. They dart about self-importantly, uttering shrill whistles, their bright red beaks thrust suddenly forward pugnaciously, or held a little to one side, as if waiting for applause. This is just a fraction of the activity which is going on continuously, so that fair weather days always seem to race by on Berneray.

This year a determined effort had been made by several voluntary work parties to get the hostel into better shape and I had thought that I might join one of these while I was here — but as with the royal visits, I arrived at the wrong time, one group had just left and another was not yet due. I'm sure I was not needed for a great deal had already been done, more even than had been planned by this stage; the building had been entirely gutted and a new roof was on and awaiting only the final thatching. It looked rather grand in its half-finished state, high and spacious with its partitions and ceilings gone. With the rough grey stone walls, lit only by a few stray gleams of daylight slanting in obliquely through the tiny windows it was rather like being in a primitive island church. The dampness had been eradicated, so as the weather continued to be very changeable I was glad to sleep inside, instead of in the tent. Since the place was officially closed I had it all to myself, which while it was convenient in the entirely open state of the building, was a pity too, for it is pleasant to have company around the fire in the evening.

One day I had tea with Roderick Macleod, who after seventeen years as the Church of Scotland minister for Berneray was about to depart to a new mainland living. We talked a little about the problems and benefits of small island life and of how things had changed in the years he had been there. Basically he thought there had been few real changes during his time, the population had continued to dwindle and there was still absolutely no work for girls on the island, so it was off to the mainland for them as soon as they had finished their schooling. Prospects were a little better for the boys with a few opportunities in the fishing line, especially now that all sorts of marine life were being harvested for export which had never before been fished — velvet crab and the hard-shelled prawns for example. Life was certainly a little more comfortable as far as material things went and the new grants had provided a mile of new township roads, ten well-designed council houses and of course the car ferry. On the debit side there was the erosion of social life caused by people staying around their television sets, instead of all the impromptu ceilidhing that used to happen. That was also partly responsible for the erosion of the Gaelic language; none of the island children used Gaelic once they had started school now, and often their parents didn't speak it either. Berneray's biggest strength he thought was its religious cohesion, all of the population except four or so being active members of the Church of Scotland, instead of being split among the nonconformists which is often the case on the other Protestant islands and which can be deeply divisive in a small community. Whatever changes were occurring, Berneray was still essentially one large family he thought and as such it was worth all the money that had been spent on it in the last few years to keep it viable.

It was the minister who seemed to do most of the organising of Berneray Week and he told me to be sure to come to the ceilidh. I needed no urging, nothing would have kept me away as I have always had a fondness for such events especially when they are staged on small islands or in other isolated communities. It is not so much the performances as the atmosphere which is so enjoyable. Everybody knows everyone else except for the handful of tourists who are politely ignored — unless they happen to be young girls, in which case all the young, unmarried men will be courting their favour, since young women are nearly always in short supply. I like the way that people just get up and sing their song or do whatever it is they are called upon to do, without any fuss or false show of reluctance. They won't have prepared anything specially but sing the traditional songs everyone knows and expects from them. There is no element of surprise or novelty for the audience, it's more like a family celebration which is enjoyed precisely because of its continuity and predictability. Sometimes the programme is stiffened up with paid performers — so that admission money can decently be charged. We had a young man from Skye who sang Gaelic songs and a couple of young girl dancers whose feet couldn't be seen as there wasn't a stage and barely enough floor space for the performers to stand in, let alone dance. The intervals were enjoyed even more for the exchange of endless gossip and listening to this I remembered what the minister had said about the vanishing Gaelic language. It certainly seemed to be only those over fifty who were not talking English. More than half the gathering no longer lived on Berneray but were expatriates whose children now had a different mother tongue. They came from as far away as Canada and the identity they were celebrating was for many of them already only a nostalgic memory.

The hall where both events were held was on its last legs. Close beside it a new hall was almost finished, paid for I was told by the islanders themselves. I expressed surprise that so few people could raise the amount of money needed and was told by the local builder that Berneray people could do anything they set their minds to 'not like that idle, drunken lot south of Benbecula'. I didn't gather why Berneray people were paying for what other islands were getting through grants, but what really matters is that the new hall is ready before they plan another film show. The one I went to had more comic value than was strictly intended and before the many holes and missing windows were blacked out sufficiently for the screen to be seen I was sure the minister would lose his balance and come crashing to the ground or that the ladder would break through the rotted floor. The electricity supply was also not totally under control so that the projector frequently changed speed or stopped altogether. But all this was as nothing compared with the disruption caused by the late arrival of a good quarter of the audience. These latecomers would stand squarely between lens and screen peering into the gloom and greeting friends, while they waited for those already seated to squeeze up closer and make room for them. We had started about an hour later than the advertised time and even an hour after that, people were still arriving for the ninety minute programme. As with the ceilidh, the main attraction was seeing friends and having 'a crack' with them, neither of which helped the barely audible sound track. The refreshment table at the back provided additional competition too, as the children constantly repaired there to buy crackly packets of crisps and cans of Coke throughout the showing.

This sort of activity can be an entertainment in itself and it made a welcome diversion to the first film shown that evening, which was about croft life on Harris during the First World War and about as far removed from reality as it is possible to get without quite entering the realms of pure fantasy. A lovely island heroine looking as though she had just stepped out of the hands of the make-up department (which I suppose she had) trips daintily through bog and heather, trilling away perpetually like a lark, while single-handed she heaves great bales of Harris tweed around — aged, white-haired mother sits helpless and decorative by her spinning wheel throughout. Young brother in the navy finds his ship torpedoed under him and makes it back to his island home — thirty days or so in an open boat and still has the strength to foot it home unaided to loving female arms. Everybody is very clean and very brave and they are ultimately rewarded by having the emblem of authentic Harris tweed stamped upon their cloth.

The film which followed was the German Count's beautiful picture of life on Eriskay in the thirties, which I wrote about earlier. Its total realism made a startling contrast to the preceeding soap opera and seemed to be about a different people living in another part of the world altogether in quite another century, instead of twenty years later as in fact it was. It was really too good a film to be subjected to such projection and I can only hope I get the chance to see it again sometime under more controlled conditions.

The main event of the evening for which everyone had come was a film about their own island, made for T.V. and called the Shepherds of Berneray. It is about shepherding in general and getting sheep off and on the uninhabited offshore islands in particular and all the characters involved are Berneray folk. I hadn't yet seen it yet but was aware of the controversy surrounding it and of the many allegations of cruelty, which I had found hard to equate with people I knew as essentially gentle and kindly. Most of the filming had been done in fairly trying weather conditions and seemed to be an honest attempt to show what such shepherding is really like. I think there was a certain amount of unintended exaggeration because of the presence of the cameras but even so I did find it a brutal and a bloody portrayal of shepherding and really quite disturbing. The sheep were handled with a violence and a disregard for their welfare that I haven't seen elsewhere, even when I've helped with gathering and shearing in wild and difficult terrain on the Scottish mainland. Allowing for the fact that the men were operating in extreme conditions, often at risk to their own lives, and with the movement of tides to consider, there still seemed to be a large measure of unnecessary violence and callousness towards the sheep. Some of the islanders themselves expressed concern over incidents in the film as did many of the expatriates who were present and some suggested that if these uninhabited islands can be grazed only by subjecting the animals to such treatment it would be better to stop it altogether — sentiments I fully share.

It was extraordinary to come out of such scenes at almost ten o'clock at night to be greeted by the most marvellous evening sky I have ever experienced even in this place of superlative skies. The light in the western sky was quite astonishing, long after the sun had set in a riot of yellow and orange hues. I can only describe it as the most unearthly sort of light I have ever seen, more like the dawning of a new world. Everyone coming out of the hall remarked upon it with gasps of amazement and delight. At 1 a.m. the afterglow was still lighting up the western sky, quite overpowering the half moon and the stars in the eastern sky — it was very difficult to tear myself away and go to bed.

As though nothing could possibly compete with such magnificence, the next two days were shrouded in mist and the island became a closed world, effectively cut off from everywhere. A grey damp world where every surface was covered with water droplets, and bird calls and the sounds of the sea came muted as though through cotton wool. It was the sort of weather that has driven many people to drink or despair, for it can last for weeks at a time and to be imprisoned in the chilly grey sameness, without a glimpse of the sun and with horizons shrunk to just a few feet all around is remarkably depressing after a while. But for just two days it had a certain Celtic charm that was not unattractive. I found the best way to stay warm and cheerful was through plenty of physical activity. There was wood to be gathered and chopped for the fire and then I chopped lots more for the next working party. When I wanted a change I rode Evans over the low hills to the machair where the cattle loomed up like monsters out of the mist, breathing out great clouds of vapour to add to the already moisture-laden air.

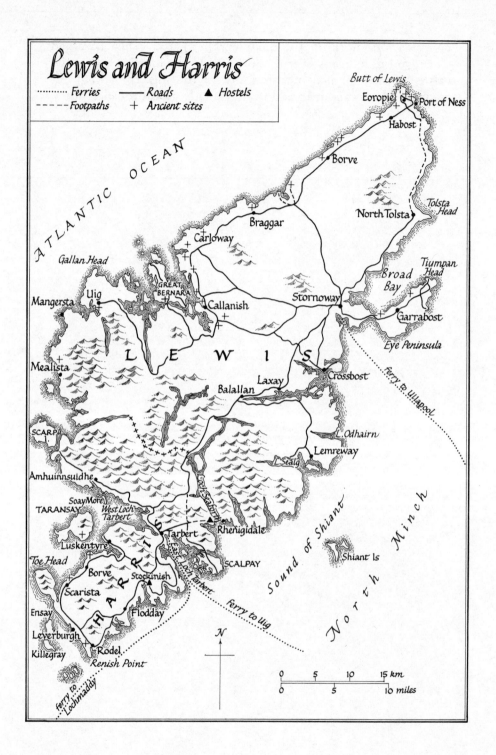

TWELVE

> North fra this Ile lyis the Harray and Leozus, quilk is
> but ane Ile baith togidder, extending in lenth fra the
> south — west to the north-east 60 miles.
>
> *Dean Munro*

> The eastern coast of Harris is generally rocky and
> mountainous, some parts of the hills are naked with-
> out earth. The west side is for the most part arable on
> the sea-coast.
>
> *Martin Martin*

T HE PASSENGER FERRY BOAT FROM
Berneray, having threaded its tortuous path through all the myriad
little islands of the Sound of Harris landed me at Leverburgh, which
is towards the south-western point of the largest and most northerly
land mass in the Outer Hebrides. As the Dean noted, Harris and
Lewis are but one island divided by a boundary composed of the
high northern hills, and the fiord-like cleft of Loch Seaforth. But
they are very different places topographically; Lewis is mostly a large
central peat moor with a little fertile land around the edges, whereas
Harris presents great contrasts between its tall stark hills and the
western seaboard of arable machair and golden beaches.

The car ferry to Harris puts in on the east coast, at Tarbert, where
the island is nipped into a waist only a few hundred yards wide,
almost riven through by the sea working away at it from both the
east and west. For nearly all first time visitors this approach to Harris
is a shock, for the sheer bleakness of the bare dark landscape, almost
devoid of vegetation takes everyone some little while to adjust to.
At first sight it appears so alien, so inhospitable that the surface of
the moon seems the only possible comparison. Going south from
Tarbert nothing relieves this first impression, if anything the land
grows even bleaker as it climbs over the edge of the South Harris
Forest — forest here means simply a treeless waste of hills given over
entirely to deer. After a few miles the ways divide, the main road

turning abruptly westward, to follow a precipitous way down a narrow glen. In the formless, chaotic landscape the road seems nothing short of a miracle, a friendly and familiar presence.

Without warning, as the road swings round what seems like just another bend in the long descent, the marvellous expanse of the sands of Luskentyre come suddenly into view. It is the most astounding and unexpected sight, as though some great force had suddenly thrust the mountains apart on either side. One moment everything is bounded by a narrow, rocky gully and in the next, a limitless ocean tumbles and breaks on the far edges of a vast golden beach: in an instant the world has changed from a silent stony desert into a veritable paradise, teeming with life and colour, birdsong, and the sound of water.

Going down the other coast of Harris, it isn't until the traveller has turned the southern point of the island and started back on the far end of the western road that the first sandy beach appears. The eastern way is all rock, and though it is called the Golden Road, this has nothing at all to do with colour, but refers to the colossal cost of constructing a path through the tortuous terrain. It follows a circuitous and mountainous course around the most spectacularly riven coastline in all the Outer Hebrides — a way more suited to mountain goats than to wheeled vehicles. Loch after loch has cut deeply into the high rocky shore and so little flat ground is there that the road having descended to sea level has immediately to climb over the next headland in a series of steep twisting curves, with hardly a straight section anywhere. It is a masterpiece of road construction and travelling it by bicycle is like riding a giant roller coaster. The only level places are the surfaces of hundreds of fresh water trout lochs and these with their summer crops of waxy white water-lilies look unbelievably opulent in the grey stony land.

Until the 19th century no-one lived on the east side of Harris, for there was not enough soil anywhere to provide even occasional pasturage for cattle; it was simply a barren waste. Yet by 1837 nearly the entire western side had been cleared for sheep and everyone who was not hounded off to America was driven on to this same coast, where, as one crofter was later to tell the commission of enquiry — 'Beasts could not live.'

Because they were not beasts, but men with no alternatives they did survive, but only by such great efforts that survival itself was a tribute to their courage and tenacity. In order to do so they had to remake the land, create places to grow their crops where there existed only unyielding stone. The women and girls trudged endlessly across the hills and up the precipitous slopes with turfs and seaweed in creels upon their backs. In small hollows between the rocks, anywhere where there was any space at all they built up the soil and constructed their so mis-named lazy beds; thousands upon thousands of them were made in this way. In them they planted their oats and potatoes, and with what fish they could get from the sea, generations of Harris folk reared their families.

'Nothing could be more moving than these lazy-beds of the Bays district of Harris,' wrote Sir Frank Fraser Darling in his West Highland Survey. 'Some no bigger than a dining table and about the same height from the ground. One of these tiny lazy-beds will yield a sheaf of oats or a bucket of potatoes, a harvest no man should despise.'

Most of these man-made fields have vanished now, but patches of heath and heather have found a foothold on the remains of them, softening the stony wilderness just a little. These are one of the people's few tangible memorials, for even their burial grounds could not be established here but had to be on the other side of Harris, where the sandy soil provides enough depth to dig a grave.

I still experience an initial sense of awe and disbelief as I'm confronted by this landscape. In spite of all his efforts, man has really left little more trace upon it than a nomadic tribe passing through. In spite of the road and the small townships huddled inconspicuously among the rocks and the few small boats in the bays, it is still essentially an unchanged primeval wilderness where man literally hasn't been able to scratch the surface. That surface is Lewisian gneiss, one of the oldest rocks on earth and it dominates everything. Nowhere else in the islands is it exposed to this degree; most places have at least the semblance of a thin covering of grass, or heath. This is like a skeleton picked clean, acres of bare stone, in sheets, boulders, cliffs and hillsides. Every living thing in that landscape, even the lichen on the rocks assumes the heightened significance and poignancy that marks life in desert places.

A barren and savage landscape it most certainly is and yet it has extraordinary beauty, once the eye had adjusted to it. It isn't all a uniform dark grey as at first appears. There is a web of soft, subtle colour, made up of tiny flowers and lichens and the gradations and shades of the rock itself. In sunlight with a dark blue sea sparkling below and the marvellous island light over everything, it is majestic. Seeing it in those conditions, I feel a tremendous sense of fulfilment just being there, as I did at my first sight of the Himalayas. I tend to think now that there is something very similar about both places, something implacable and shorn of extraneous matter, that has the power to release people from their own petty concerns.

I came here first, fifteen years ago to spend a few days walking up the coast with my three young children. We had always spent the long summer holidays in a rented cottage on Skye or in remote places on the north-western coast and often on fine days we had seen these far islands of the Outer Hebrides beckoning like sirens from across the Minch. One year when we were holidaying at no great distance from the Uig ferry on Skye, we had responded to a sudden impulse, packed our sleeping bags, cooking things and a couple of mountain tents and had taken the boat over to Tarbert. Although the children were well used to wild country by this time and were looking forward to the expedition, Harris brought them up with a jolt, intimidating them with its grey severity. But by the end of that first sunny day they had been thoroughly won over, as I was, and were no longer comparing it with the surface of the moon.

We had gone by bus down the west side to Rodel, at the southern extremity, and we'd walked back over three days, along the Golden Road, exploring each bay and little fishing hamlet which the road links. The weather had been kind to us until the last morning, and the Harris folk had been even kinder. Every vehicle that came along — possibly one an hour — stopped to see if we wanted a lift. In every village people had tried to take us in and feed us. The children who had less inhibitions than I, and were endlessly hungry in the sea air, ate countless meals of fresh eggs and scones, ignoring my instructions to say, 'No thank you.' Children and young people were clearly a scarcity among the ageing population and my town-reared 'nuclear' family revelled in all the unaccustomed attention as of a vast extended family which was showered upon them. Everyone we met seemed so pleased that we found their island worth visiting and equally surprised that we were prepared to sleep in tents 'like tinks' when they would certainly have found a space for us in their cottages.

The only way I could make any recompense for all this kindness was by buying items of the women's knitting which were put out for sale on chairs at the cottage doors. As I was the main load bearer of the party I wasn't all that keen on acquiring extra weight but I never regretted the items I bought. The sweaters and stockings knitted in the hard hairy local wool proved to be almost waterproof and virtually indestructible. We'd seen women walking back from the peat banks knitting as they went, the balls of wool tucked under their arms, though mostly they built up their stocks in the long dark winter evenings. The women have learnt to knit their complicated patterns — very like the Aran style, by feel and memory so it was a good activity for dimly lit cottages in a season when there was little to be done outside.

I find the Golden Road little changed since that first visit. There is the occasional newly-built, self-conscious looking bungalow with nameplates like 'Four Winds' or 'View of Skye' — hardly necessary really considering the prevalence of both views and wind. A few more old cottages have become holiday homes; purchased mainly by Germans, who are prone to becoming addicted to the Outer Hebrides and have more money than most to maintain a place so far away. There are a rather more cars about and empty half whisky bottles and beer cans are discarded more thickly along the roadside now perhaps, though these last have always been plentiful. There are so few places to drink, especially on Harris and Lewis and the men take 'carry-outs' when they leave the bars and presumably finish the bottles in their vehicles on these lonely twisting roads. I have seen women working at the peats, smashing these empty whisky bottles for no reason that I can make out, other than resentment or profound dislike of what they once contained. For the sake of their animals' feet and of my tyres I wish they'd express their displeasure some other way. As for the effect of this roadside drinking on the quality of the driving, I haven't heard that there are many accidents but I make sure I'm never bicycling after dark, at least not on those tortuous bends.

The only youth hostel on the Outer Hebrides, until the Gatliffe Trust was established and the Loch Maddy hostel was opened recently, was on this coast, at a village just to the north of the Bays area, called Stockinish. As there is hardly anywhere else to stay on this side of Harris, it is nearly always well filled with an international crowd of all ages and can have a tremendous atmosphere. It is housed in the old village school, minimally converted to provide the basic conditions that my generation of hostellers grew up to accept as the norm. I've always been grateful for an early introduction to rugged living as it has held me in good stead in my later travels in primitive places. People with a less Spartan background can be devastated when they arrive at somewhere like Stockinish and if weather conditions are poor the atmosphere can deteriorate quite badly.

The washing facilities — cold taps only or boil a kettle of hot water to take in with you — are in outbuildings in the playground. The only heating in the single common room/kitchen/dining room comes from a tiny stove that can't possibly cope with drying the wet clothing of two dozen hostellers. I've been here when there was twice that number — sleeping like sardines all over the floor, because the weather had been so awful that people couldn't with humanity be turned away. It says a great deal about the appeal of the Outer Hebrides that many people not only survive these conditions but return again and again when for half the cost they could be lying in hot sun on a Mediterranean beach.

There are almost no B&B places on this side of Harris in spite of extensive efforts on the parts of the Tourist Board and others, to persuade local people to earn a little extra cash by providing the much needed accommodation. Part of the reason for this is undoubtedly due to religion. If Sunday didn't exist, life would be far less problematical on this island. On Saturday night the few B&B boards that there are, are covered over with sacking; doors are closed and no-one emerges again, except to go to the kirk, until after 12 p.m. Sunday night. If you fall off your bicycle on Sunday, I'm pretty sure it would be Monday before anyone picked you up. Even ten years ago I've seen cockerels imprisoned under lobster creels all day Sunday, in case they defiled the Sabbath by treading hens. I have even been 'called after' by an old woman who saw me riding one Sunday. 'The Lord sees all,' she shouted at my offending back. This was funny really because this same old woman had deliberately cheated me out of a small sum of money the day before, when I had called to collect the socks she had persuaded me into letting her knit. We had already agreed the price but she doubled it, over a cup of tea, depending upon my embarrassment not to protest. A neighbour of hers told me later that this was her usual practice; she said that the woman's knitting was so poor that she had to get double money for it because no-one came to her a second time.

We were all very careful at the hostel to try not to offend against Sabbath observance. No washing was left out drying on the lines on Sunday — something considered particularly heinous, and people were asked not to leave or arrive on that day (the ferries didn't run anyway so you couldn't have left the island). But you couldn't expect people to stay indoors, especially in fine weather. As the Free Church religion sees its responsibility extending to 'the stranger at the gate', who should be made to tow the line just as it says in

Exodus, 'Ye shall have one manner of law for the stranger, as for one of your own country' no totally satisfactory solution is possible. By and large however, a compromise was reached, foreigners were simply ignored on Sundays as if they didn't exist. If the islanders in their black clothes going to and fro from the three long kirk services caught sight of you, they simply turned their backs, even folk who had shared a cup of tea with you the day before. It was embarrassing and very sad.

There could be embarrassments on the other side too sometimes; maybe a daughter emancipated by life on the mainland was home for the weekend to straighten up the place a bit for an aged parent. If it was an isolated cottage she might risk shaking out a rug or two between services, only to find herself caught in the act by someone passing the house. Only a tourist! But it might have been a church elder. There always seemed to me a sound of desperation as the person hurried inside and slammed the door — public reproval of such offenders was a common occurrence of Sunday services.

I have no great affection for the Free Church, for it seems to me that it binds Christianity in a straight-jacket of Old Testament judgemental fundamentalism — harsh, implacable and self-righteous. It parallels the same intolerant attitudes that are displayed by Moslem extremists or the Ultra-Orthodox Jews of Jerusalem and operates far more by fear than by love. All three of these expressions of religion insist upon their obligation to bring the rest of the world into line with their minority views. I cannot see that this kind of Old Testament fundamentalism is in keeping either with the basic tenets of Christianity itself or with the kindly gentle temperament of Hebridean people. It is an attitude that has much to answer for; it is now generally accepted that it was the repressive practices of the Free Church that in no small part contributed to the final collapse and evacuation of the St. Kilda community. It undermined the culture and sapped much of the islanders' spontaneous joy in living. Their traditional outlets for recreation, like dancing and singing were discouraged as 'sinful' and 'works of the devil' and the incredibly long services and prayer meetings they were made to attend seriously affected the pursuit of their livelihood. More importantly it helped to erode their belief in themselves, and in their unique way of life.

Like many religious systems which have subsequently become constricting influences, the Free Church arose at a time of unrest and was at the centre of a popular movement for social change and justice. The actual founding of the Free Church — known as the Disruption of the Church of Scotland — happened in 1843 when the internecine wrangling between Moderates and Evangelicals led to the latter's secession. But evangelicism was already firmly established in the northern part of the Outer Hebrides, having come there hard on the heels of the spread of literacy. Until about 1800 few people could read and the majority were dependent for their knowledge of the Bible on the clergy of the Established Church. They alone had access to sources and their interpretations of scripture were therefore impossible to refute. After 1800 all that changed. The Gaelic translation of the Bible appeared in 1801 and over the next 25 years 140,000 copies were distributed throughout the Highlands and Islands by SSPCK and the British and Foreign Bible Society. The Gaelic School Society was founded in 1811 and the only book used in their schools was the Gaelic Bible.

Religious fervour swept through the islands. A people whose lives are so desperately hard in this world are ripe for evangelising in preparation for the next. Literacy added a new dimension to the work and was a powerful weapon for a down-trodden peasantry, not least in the discovery that the ministers of the Established Church could now be seen as not necessarily infallible. There was ample material in the Bible, especially in the Old Testament that the crofting community could apply directly to their own situation, particularly in relation to the land of which they had been robbed.

The Established Church was not slow to see the danger even if there was little they could do to avert it. Gaelic Society teachers began to set themselves up as preachers in direct opposition to the ministers. They urged the people to shun church services, claiming that the Gospel was not preached there. Landlords were equally aware of the danger; the French Revolution was far too recent an event for complacency. As the Evangelical movement spread and the parish churches stood empty, they refused to sell land for the building of the rival churches. Since all the land was owned by landlords, in some islands it was possible to prevent the Society's presence altogether, and in many places it was made extremely difficult for the services to be held anywhere, even in the fields. All this was grist to the Evangelical mill of course — religion thrives on persecution. But as a traveller of that time noted, it was as much a social as a religious issue, a matter of rich and poor; landed and landless.

Out of this turbulent climate came the new phenomenon of the lay preacher, possibly the most significant event in the revivalist movement. These preachers — known as *na daoine*, the men, to distinguish them from ordained ministers, were the first leaders to arise from the ranks of the crofters. There had been earlier precedents for 'the men' since Covenanting days but it was not until the 19th century that they gained their immense influence. The sort of huge revivalist meetings they conducted, particularly on Fridays before a communion service, are not so common any longer, not at least in this country; though they still occur frequently in some parts of the world, particularly in the emergent nations. According to eye witnesses they were scenes, of wild religious ecstasy, where visions and prophesies, fits and convulsions, screaming, wailing and gnashing of teeth were all quite commonplace. The style of preaching of 'the men' was of the exhortation variety, full of personal wrestling with the Devil and his minions. They knew their Bible as only people who read nothing else can know it, literally word for word. It was the Revealed Word of God and did not brook interpretation. This rigid, unquestioning belief, combined often with ancient pre-Christian gifts of second sight and mystical powers was a strong and persuasive force. It was small wonder that many of these men's congregations considered them prophets and believed in their abilities to confer curses and blessings.

After the Disruption, 'the men' became absorbed into the now official and dominant Free Church and their influence continued; indeed in some instances it doesn't seem any weaker than it was two hundred years ago. Some enjoy an exercise of power that can overturn the wishes and desires of the majority as in the case of Sunday ferries on neighbouring Skye, also a Free Church stronghold. After an opinion poll had decided overwhelmingly in favour of all-week access, the ferry ran on the Sabbath. The result was dramatic. Mr. Smith the Free Church minister lay down on the slipway in front of the cars. The police eventually carried him off, but the attempt to operate the ferry on the Sabbath was discontinued and hasn't yet been resumed. At one of the rare cinemas in Lewis the film *Jesus Christ Super Star* was shown in spite of the minister's disapproval. The manager was solemnly cursed and within weeks the cinema was closed down, on the pretext that fire regulations were being infringed.

Seen from the outside the situation is not without a degree of humour. Ministers laying curses on those who flout their authority does seem too bizarre to be believable in the cyncial urban atmosphere of the 20th century. It is nevertheless still practised even on incomers who are not part of the Free Church at all. Someone I know on Harris had their roof solemnly cursed by a Free Church minister after he had ordered them to come down off it on the Sabbath. They had been taking advantage of the first fine day to replace some missing slates and not unnaturally they declined to comply. A Roman Catholic priest who was staying with them at the time said he would bless the roof and they could wait and see who would win — that was several years ago and the roof hasn't blown off yet.

The overwhelming conviction of being the mouthpiece of the Almighty can also operate in a manner I consider little short of demonic. Only a few months ago at the burial service of a young man killed on a motor bike, the minister preached to the mourners (who included the boy's parents) that the young man would burn in everlasting hell-fire because he had been breaking the Law of God at the time of his death. I don't know what he was supposed to have done, other than having his girl friend on the back of the bike, but I think even a Free Church minister would need more evidence of sin than that to condemn a young man to eternal damnation.

All the casual visitor sees of the effect of a Free Church Sabbath, apart from the turned backs is the complete shut down of the islands' few amenities. So that from it being merely difficult to procure a drink or a meal or some petrol, on Sunday it becomes almost impossible. North of the Benbecula dividing line on a Saturday night the wise visitor is either safely ensconced with friends or cocooned in one of the few hotels that offer all amenities.

Having written so much about how the negative and repressive side of religion strikes the traveller in the northern half of the Outer Hebrides, I feel I must also recount an incident which was entirely the opposite and one of the most 'religious' encounters I have had anywhere. It happened on a summer Sunday on Lewis, the staunchest stronghold of the Free Church faith. It was a day of almost magical perfection, with no wind and clear blue skies. Since early morning I had ridden along a sparsely populated stretch of the western coast, beside superb coves and great expanses of shining sands. Every beach was deserted, for the God-fearing folk were all inside as was required of them when not at church; the children too having to sit there all day, doing nothing. I know what torture this can be for an active child, for I was subjected to the same sort of Sunday when I was evacuated to South Wales in the war. The only sure sign I'd had all day that I was not alone in this island paradise was the occasional twitch of a net curtain as I passed a house.

About tea time, as I rode through a village street where each house stood shuttered and stiff with unspoken disapproval, two old ladies appeared at their open front door smiling and beckoning. I was as surprised at this sudden appearance of friendly humanity on the Sabbath as I was the day a helicopter landed on a lonely Highland road just in front of me, the pilot having run out of petrol. Neither events had happened to me before nor have they occurred again. I stopped and the old ladies came down the garden path to the gate, still smiling and one of them said, 'You'll be thirsty with all that riding in the heat. Come away in and take a cup of tea.'

I sat with them for about an hour over the ample tea they prepared for me, while they urged me to take more. When I'd finished they asked if I would mind them turning on the wireless, because it was their favourite programme — Gaelic hymn singing they called it, but I think it was the metrical psalms, which is the only form of music in the Free Church. It is a strange sound with a lot of freedom of performance and it changes key in the oddest places. I suppose it is essentially a primitive style with a strong emotional appeal, an atavistic sort of music that makes some dogs lift up their throats and howl as though in memory of their distant wild past. I like the sound and listening to it in company with these saintly old ladies, who seemed to be delighted to have me there, I had a sense of being accepted into a special sort of fellowship as simple and holy as the breaking of bread.

CHAPTER

THIRTEEN

> Within the south part of this said Ile lyis ane Monastery with ane steipill, quhilk was foundit and biggit by Mc Cloyd of Haray callit Roadill.
>
> *Dean Munro*

> The air is temperately cold and the natives endeavour to qualify it by taking a dose of aquavitae or brandy.
>
> *Martin Martin*

AT THE END OF THE GOLDEN ROAD lies Rodel whose green luxuriance and air of faded gentility comes as a delightful surprise after all the miles of precipitous grey gneiss. This was once one of the richest farms of Harris and its verdant green acres, degenerated now to mainly rough pasture could probably produce more than the whole of the east coast put together. It is an apt setting for the one architectural gem of the Outer Hebrides — the church of St. Clements. The Cathedral of the Isles as it was known, was built in about 1500 AD, by the island's owner, the 8th MacLeod of Dunvegan and subsequently the chiefs of the MacLeod clan were buried there. There is nothing at all like it anywhere else in the Isles, a small, beautifully proportioned cruciform church with a tall square tower; built in a lovely green sandstone shipped over from Mull. The interior is simple and unfurnished, with bare stone walls and a light that looks as though it filters in through water. The only decoration is the founder's tomb, where his stone effigy is set under a carved, arched recess, decorated with fine, Celtic carvings of galleons, angels and scenes from scripture. There is also a very unusual, early stone crucifix found during the restoration work, so weathered that its simple lines could pass for a work of modern impressionism. During the last restoration in 1873, some other statuary found in the vicinity was set into the exterior walls of the tower. Strange, ancient pieces these, which look almost pre-Christian, though they could conceivably be from early tombstones of the chiefs. They are of great interest but are set too high to examine properly. It seems a very odd place to have put them, but then the Victorians had very definite ideas about their right to do as they pleased when spending their own money, and never considered themselves accountable for what they altered or destroyed during their restorations of buildings.

The tower can be climbed by a series of stairs and ladders and good views obtained of the immediate surroundings. There are no distant vistas because the whole area is well sheltered on all sides by higher ground, which must have contributed greatly to its prosperity. Shelter, especially from the prevailing westerly winds makes a tremendous difference to growing anything on these storm-harried islands. From the battlements the pleasant little valley has a decided 18th century appearance which is further enhanced by the walled graveyard full of fine Georgian tombs, also unique in the islands. Great fuschia bushes and the occasional rare tree have taken over some of these tombs and split their masonry, which together with the close mown grass and unaccustomed neatness adds to the feeling of being in a carefully contrived 18th century setting, complete with ruins.

Nearby is a splendid small harbour with wide, grass-grown quays and nothing at all in its calm waters except a rusted old fishing boat. It was constructed in the 1770s by a Captain Macleod who was in the East India trade and who had bought the farm with the idea of settling here and creating the sort of ordered existence Dr. Johnson so approved of wherever he came across it on his Hebridean Tour — which was all too rarely. This island proprietor seems to have been a model of energy and innovation — the 18th century ideal of the all-round man, educated in the arts and sciences and conversant with all the new technology. He had deepened and improved the small, well-sheltered bay and constructed a harbour where ships could lie at all states of the tide, with a graving bank at one side for repairs. His comfortable Georgian house he had directed to be set squarely at the head of the little basin where he could survey all the comings and goings from its windows. Warehouses, boat-houses, sheds and outbuildings were added; the church was restored, cart tracks constructed, trees planted and no doubt, all sorts of improved stock were introduced and new methods of agriculture foisted on a reluctant tenantry. He also found fish in great quantities where the locals claimed there were none, but in spite of all his energy and vision, he had no more success in establishing a thriving fishing industry than had the luckless Charles I before him.

I'm glad it was not this attractive 18th century man who was responsible for all the misery inflicted upon the islanders in the clearances. That was the responsibility of Macleod of Dunvegan and his rapacious factor Duncan Stewart. The final evictions which completed the depopulation of the west coast were carried out by the Earl of Dunmore, who bought Harris from the Macleods in the 1830s and took over Rodel House. The Dunmores sold out to Lord Leverhulme in 1919 and he too lived in the Captain's house for a short while, before moving up the coast to Borve. In 1923 when Lord Leverhulme's Hebridean dream had collapsed and all his assets were sold, Rodel House became an hotel, complete with most of its Edwardian trappings, and I don't think it changed one jot after that, but just very slowly decayed. I was lucky enough to have had a meal there with the children of that first visit, when it was still operating unchanged and we were shown over the place. The youngest of the children clutched my hand tightly as we were led through what seemed an endless succession of dark, gloomy corridors, dank conservatories and ante-rooms, which had been tacked on in Victorian times. The house was clearly not totally watertight by then and smelt of stone that never quite dried out. It was distinctly threadbare in places too, but the whole place was nonetheless wonderfully redolent of its expansive Edwardian period when it had played host to a succession of tweed clad gentlemen, armed with rod, line, rifle and shotgun on their annual orgy of slaughter.

Soon after the mid-nineteenth century, sheep farms had ceased to be a paying proposition and had been widely replaced by grouse moors, deer forests, and carefully maintained salmon and trout lochs. With a generation of newly-rich Victorian manufacturers eager to follow the gentlemanly pursuits of the river and the chase, wild acres of marginal land could now yield their owners fat profits from shooting and fishing rents. The decorations of Rodel Hotel bore testimony to the success of the sportsmen and their ghillies; the walls bristled with antlers, and stuffed fish and birds in cracked glass cases stared out with unblinking glassy eyes from the tops of damp-buckled tallboys, permanently coated with a film of crumbling plaster. The rooms were furnished with well-worn Edwardian furniture — solid mahogany everywhere, even around the baths and covering the loos. I don't remember what we ate at dinner, only that the china was also Edwardian and the eight-year-old could hardly manage the heavy cutlery. It was (and still is) one of the few places outside Buckingham Palace where Buchanan's Royal Household whisky can be drunk and it was my favourite hotel, although I never actually stayed there and now I've left it too late to do so because this year it is going to be extensively renovated and brought into line with 20th century expectations. I comfort myself with the thought that whatever is done to the building, its setting will always be one of the finest in the Outer Hebrides.

From Rodel to where the ferry from Berneray set me down at Leverburgh is only a couple of miles, but what a contrast in styles it presents. When I scrambled ashore up the barnacle encrusted steps, rain was falling gently, which does nothing to improve the seedy little town. It was looking even shabbier than usual, being in the middle of an extensive patching up process. The row of council houses on the main street appeared to have been attacked by a fearsome fungus, but on closer inspection I could see it was just that rotted planks had been replaced here and there and it was awaiting a coat of paint to restore it all to one colour. These particular houses are an eyesore at the best of times, straight lines don't suit the island style and they are uncompromisingly uniform. For some reason they are also enormously high and must be an awful job to heat, as well as presenting an unnecessarily large area to the battering of western gales. In a treeless habitat where timber rots easily it would also seem the height of folly to have faced them with wooden planking.

But then the whole place is a folly, a 20th century folly with none of the frivolity and elegance of the 18th century kind. I had never found anything good about Leverburgh on any occasion I'd passed through; there wasn't even a shed to shelter in while waiting for the ferry in the rain. The local shop was one of the worst I'd come across too, it would either close the moment you arrived at the door or sell you meat that was weighed and wrapped up before you could catch a glimpse of it and when you came to cook it, you found that it was all skin, bone and gristle and useless for anything except rendering down for glue. It was a town that had failed before it had ever become established, and there was no reason for it being there except for one man's dreams.

Leverburgh was renamed in honour of Lord Leverhume, before that it was an insignificant little fishing hamlet called Obbe. Lord Leverhume came here in 1919, intent on revitalising the island's economy with the fortune he'd made in soap. He was a man who combined a talent for making money with the enlightened and philanthropic ideas of the late-Victorian age. At Port Sunlight he had built a model town for his workers that seemed a veritable paradise compared with the conditions suffered by most factory workers and their families at that time, and he had been elevated to the peerage in the process. His intention was to create similar benefits for the people of Harris by organising a fishing industry but his schemes met with no more success than had those of his predecessors. It was Lewis that he'd originally intended to develop but had met such implacable hostility from the crofters there that he'd shifted his sphere of operations to Harris. He should have learnt from that first defeat and cut his losses.

There was less direct opposition here, but neither was there the whole hearted co-operation that was necessary in order to get his schemes working. Harris was not Port Sunlight and Harris people were not it seemed to be won over by model housing and other modern benefits. Lord Leverhume was a man with drive and talent, but not blessed it would seem with any great historical understanding, or an appreciation of other people's passions and differences. The last hundred and fifty years of grim struggle and privation had left the people of the Outer Hebrides with a hunger for land which only the land itself could assuage. They saw the possession of a croft as the answer to all their ills. With enough land to work they assumed that they would once again have the good life enjoyed by their forefathers. That past life-style had probably grown ever more golden in their minds as their own material conditions had worsened. Until every man had been given the piece of land he'd been promised following the 1886 Crofting Act, no-one was in any mood to pay attention to anything else. When Lord Leverhume arrived on the scene those promises had still not been totally realised and the 'Land Wars' were still being fought. The islanders had also developed an inherent distrust of landed gentry, who for so long had been benefiting from what they believed was rightfully theirs, while they struggled and starved on barren rock. Many of them seemed to have seen Lord Leverhume's project not as a potential benefit, but as a threat, another attempt to deprive them of their land. He was a man who was there at the wrong time, though whether there would ever have been a right time for his ideas is doubted by most authorities. When his schemes failed and his island estates were sold off in 1923 everything went for a song. He had lost a fortune and there was nothing to show for it but this ugly little town. I think Captain

Macleod of Rodel fared more happily and certainly left a more beautiful memorial.

There had been changes at Leverburgh since my last visit. Apart from the parti-coloured council houses, several other houses were having a face-lift and there was even one new functional building. This housed a really good supermarket, a craft centre and a café selling homemade cakes and cups of tea and was run by the island co-operative. I didn't stop to take advantage of these improvements since I was bound for Scarista, a few miles further on where there was (until this latest rival appeared) the only café south of Tarbert and almost the only place in the entire Outer Hebrides where you could enjoy real coffee. It also sold teas other than Indian, homemade soup, salads, and cakes that were truly memorable. This fare, as delectable as it is rare in those parts, was served in a small white room where the walls were hung with paintings which I also looked forward to seeing, in fact I enjoyed the whole place. It was the home of the artist David Miles, his wife Janet and their two teenage children, a small house that you squeezed down the side of, between the stone wall of the cottage and a narrow stream thickly overhung by young sycamores — a rare sight in the treeless isles. The café was tacked on at the back, overlooking a small garden which was yet another delight and revelation as to what flowers and vegetables could do in this shallow sandy soil, with a little shelter and a dressing of rotted seaweed from the shore.

Food always seems to be a pre-occupation when it is hard to come by, or of limited variety; and in a place like the Outer Hebrides, which is teeming with delicious seafood, succulent lamb, venison, salmon, trout and so forth, to have to make do with frozen and convenience food is particularly trying. But after some weeks of eating little which does not taste of monosodium glutamate, what I long for most is not the rare and exotic, but simple fresh vegetables. So having anticipated this treat for some time, to arrive at Scarista Studio and find it closed was galling, so much so that I had the temerity to ring the door bell, just in case someone had forgotten to change the 'Closed' sign to 'Open'. This was in fact the case and I was welcomed in, but instead of just having a meal and going on my way, Janet Miles and I got talking and found we had so much we wanted to discuss, that I ended up staying there as her guest for the next few days — very exhausting days they were too, as we talked on into the small hours and in the daytime I attempted to help with the café.

Janet had come to the Outer Hebrides with another young art

student twenty years before, to spend a summer vacation painting. The two girls had arrived in Tarbert and enquired at the Post Office as to where they were likely to find a cheap house for rent. The post master had suggested the small island of Scarp, lying a hundred yards off the northwest coast of Harris. They had duly gone there, found an empty house and painted hard all summer; helping the locals with harvest work between times. They must have been a tremendous attraction to the young men who were not only deprived of young Scarp women — most of whom would be away working on the mainland, but who would also have found London art students quite exotic in pretelevision days. As a result they were well looked after, taken on lots of fishing trips and given a good introduction to island life. David who had recently met Janet and who was already a working painter had come up to see her at the end of the summer and they had returned together on a lobster fishing boat which was sailing down the west coast of Harris, lifting its creels as it made its slow way to Oban. Having only seen the rocky scenery of the islands up till then, the miles of deserted sandy beaches along this Atlantic seaboard of Harris were a revelation to them both and it seems to me they fell in love with it as they were falling in love with each other. Within a year they were back for another painting trip. This time the same obliging post master was asked to suggest where they might find a house beside a sandy beach and he told them to contact a certain crofter at Scarista. They spent that night on the beach and the following day they met the crofter as arranged and found themselves not the tenants but the owners of a very small, three-roomed house, with a bit of land at the rear and a short stretch of machair between it, and one of the loveliest beaches of Harris.

As Janet sees it, it all happened simply and naturally with no real decision making on their part. Harris was the right place for them and the house had been there, furnished and equipped down to the last teaspoon, all for two hundred pounds. There had been no bargaining, it was just assumed that they would buy it and the Miles had seen no reason why they shouldn't. However, it was more money than they actually possessed and David had to spend the first winter scenery painting in London theatres, while Janet moved in and produced their first child. Her fellow student of the Scarp painting trip also settled in the Outer Hebrides, on North Uist.

David and Janet's only home ever since has been Harris; and they have never thought of it as just a base, or a holiday home. They've established their roots here and raised and educated their two children, the elder of whom, like any other island child has already gone to make her life elsewhere. The house has grown from its original three small rooms, expanding upwards and outwards to accommodate the family's growing needs. It is a very unselfconscious house and strictly practical; there is nothing about it that has been altered other than for reasons of utility, for David does all the alterations himself and resents unecessary time taken away from painting. It has everything needed for convenience and comfort without the gadgetry and clutter that is becoming such a feature of modern homes and can be so time consuming to maintain. Not unnaturally, considering they are both artists it is also a very attractive place — yet another island home I could happily live in.

I didn't meet David because he was away painting in Italy but I was glad of the opportunity of a closer acquaintance with his pictures. Much of his work is an exploration of Harris, of its textures, light, moods and colour. Having the opportunity to live with the paintings while I was immersed in the same landscape deepened my appreciation and understanding of both. There are several artists and potters on the Outer Hebrides producing really fine and exciting things, but working up here out of the main swing of the art world, few of them get much recognition or find it easy to make a living — which of course is nothing new for artists and not to be wondered at really. If artists see a little more or a bit further than the rest of humanity, then tastes have to have time to catch up with their vision. Most people prefer not to be stretched too far and relate best to art that is well established and a safe investment. If a modern artist wants much success in his lifetime he has to be prepared to put a lot of effort into promoting his work and that means spending time in cities, particularly London and New York. For an artist whose inspiration is found in the Outer Hebrides this is not an attractive idea. The compensations for the lack of recognition are obviously worth it or such places would not attract so many creative people — unless it is that such artists have no choice and have to be where their inspiration is. Most of the island artists must of necessity find an additional source of income. David is lucky that Janet puts his work before her own and helps make ends meet with the café and some art teaching in the island schools. They also turn out good replicas of the delightful Norse chess set which was found in Lewis and is now in the British Museum, and also a few figurines of islanders engaged in traditional pursuits to sell to the café customers.

At first I thoroughly enjoyed the novelty of waiting upon the few customers, it was a treat to see their surprise at being served such unexpectedly good things, just as I had been on my first visit. I kept hoping that one of them would buy a painting, but they never did, though quite a few of the figurines were sold and a complete chess set. Janet said the best patrons tended to be Scandinavians as they knew how to look at paintings whereas she felt that this was not a common attribute of the British. The enjoyment of serving in a café didn't last very long, in fact it vanished when we were honoured with the custom of a shopkeeper from Stornoway who arrived on the Sabbath with his own wine, a friend and two young women, all of whom were already the worse for drink and got steadily noisier and more inebriated at the hours passed and they sat on and on over their homemade soup and pizzas, long since grown cold and gelid. Fortunately no other customers turned up, but the frequent thuds and bangs proceeding from behind the closed door of the little room had us concerned for the safety of the paintings. It was difficult for Janet to suggest to them that they had overstayed their welcome since she knew the shopkeeper, who was apparently, a perfectly mild-mannered soul when not under the influence of the demon drink. Nothing was damaged fortunately, and they left of their own accord, though it was alarming to think of them driving the sixty winding miles back to Stornoway in that state.

The café was never so busy that my presence was any real benefit nor was my lifting the daily quota of potatoes and other vegetables from the fruitful little garden anything other than a delightful chore for me. There was however one function for which I was indispensable and that was driving the Miles' eccentric little Citroen car. Janet could drive but didn't have a licence, Reuben her sixteen year-old son, who was very mechanically minded, could also drive but wasn't allowed to, being under age. So with David away, in order to visit the bar at Rodel or to attend any functions too far to walk to, it had to be me at the wheel, since I had both the skill and the licence. The Miles' car was no sinecure, being old enough to have developed the crotchety eccentricities which only an owner of long standing can easily cope with. I needed Reuben with me in order to get me over these, and to repair things that went wrong or fell off — like the accelerator linkage. It had the weirdest gear shift too, which went from fourth to second with great ease, missing out third which one had been aiming for. Each rasping mis-change elicited a groan from Reuben who really liked machinery and hated to hear it abused. On the rare occasions when I got it right, I earned sarcastic applause. I curried favour by letting him reverse the car when it was necessary to do so, a manoeuvre he performed with great panache and adroitness. Even so he still insisted I was to blame whenever we had to stop for him to reassemble the throttle linkage; he said it only fell off because I wriggled my foot about. One night we stopped at the top of a steep slope, the linkage again in pieces because I'd pushed my foot almost through the floorboards in an effort to get the reluctant machine over the crest of the hill. While Reuben and a friend of his muttered and groaned under the bonnet trying to effect a repair in the light of the dimmest little torch I'd ever seen, Janet and I gazed over the Scarista sands where a huge yellow moon hung low above a calm sea. The contrast between the scene of niggling mechanical minutiae and the glorious natural world all around had us simultaneously reduced to near hysteria.

We were in need of some such relief having had a very trying evening, watching five hours of a home video about a wedding that had been celebrated at the lovely Rodel Church the day before I arrived. One of the guests had made the film, a young man in his early thirties from Edinburgh, called Angus, who had been left enough money so that he did not have to work and could buy himself lots of gadgetry such as the video camera. Strictly speaking the film was really about Angus's attendance at the wedding — all three days of it, rather than about the wedding itself. It began as soon as the boat arrived at Stornoway and continued blow by blow, every inch of the sixty miles down the coast, the camera strapped into the passenger seat and Angus's monotonous voice lecturing about the countryside. No boring detail, whether of filling up with petrol or eating lunch was omitted. Very soon it was clear that it wasn't meant to be some juvenile attempt at humour but was deadly serious. There were a lot of people assembled to watch; those who were stationed near the door managed to leave very early on, the host also vanished and was found later in another room fast asleep. The rest of us had no opportunity for escape and stayed grimly with it, an unwilling, captive audience. We had Angus going to bed, Angus getting up and donning his kilt; even Angus in church singing a hymn, competing with the minister whose voice rose and fell and changed key as often as was necessary in order to be heard above the other voices. Occasionally there were shots of the bride and groom and other guests but mostly it was upon Angus himself that the camera was focused. At one stage, while he was threading up yet another reel, his brother said with great satisfaction, 'It's already longer than *The Sound of Music*. I think we should propose a vote of thanks to Angus for a really splendid effort.' We'd about got to the wedding dinner speeches by that time and thanks to a general stretching of legs Janet and I were able to make our escape.

By way of compensation we spent the following evening in the bar at Rodel, where a mixture of incomers, visitors and islanders seemed to be getting on very well together except for one local man. 'Tourists,' he said in great disgust, 'are taking over from the sheep in ruining this island. Harris should be for Harris people we could solve our own problems without help from anyone.' This seemed to me a sour remark especially considering how much today's incomers contribute to the life of these islands, with their new ideas and energy. Even visitors have their uses, apart from the money which the tourist trade produces; like the big Canadian hitch-hiker drinking quietly at the bar, who was well into his second month on Harris. He was a stone mason, who having been given a lift by a recent white settler had stayed to help put a new roof on the settler's house. Already he'd had offers from other island folk wanting to hire his skills and he could have stayed there as long as he'd wished and made a steady living. People like the Miles who quietly get on with their lives and at the same time offer a much needed service to visitors seem to me to have as much right to be there as the indigenous folk. Indeed on the grounds that those who make the best use of the land have the most right to it, the bare unworked crofts could hardly be offered as an argument against the incomers gardens with their crops of vegetables, flowers and trees.

From earliest times there has been constant change in these islands, new blood coming in, new peoples displacing the old or being absorbed by them. Not for nothing have the Outer Hebrides been called the Islands of the Strangers. All these different peoples played their part in evolving a method of husbandry which once existed here, where people and land were in harmony. The necessities of life were grown without undue toil and a natural surplus of cattle was produced for trade; the cattle being an important element in maintaining the ground's fertility. Somehow the population also managed to maintain itself at a healthy level without overcrowding, as Martin Martin observed around 1700 A.D.

'If any family, reduced to low circumstances, had a mind to retire to any of these Isles, there is no part of the known world where they may have the products of sea and land cheaper, live more securely, or among a more tractable and mild people. And that the country in general is healthful, appears from the good state of health enjoyed by the inhabitants.'

Soon after he wrote that everything changed, with the exploitation of the land for the benefit of the very few. The most energetic islanders left of their own accord to colonise other lands, not waiting for the later evictions. The most successful island children found their futures away from their birthplace. Those left behind had little but poverty to look forward to and the essential harmony between the land and the people was irretrievably broken.

The granting of crofts didn't reverse this trend, partly because by that time conditions throughout Britain had changed and higher material expectations had made crofting no longer seem such an attractive way of life. To a large extent the dream was over before it had ever really begun — island self-sufficiency in the early 20th century was at best a touch and go possibility, no matter how much it was artificially propped up. Subsidies have become a way of life in farming everywhere now in the E.E.C. but whether they are *per se* a good thing is disputable, and we might do well to ask ourselves what benefits are conferred by butter and beef mountains, wine lakes and so forth. We can go on artificially preserving a life-style in the Outer Hebrides by pouring in money I suppose, but whether it will actually maintain anything other than the mere shell of that life is very doubtful; the basis for preserving any way of life must surely have some relation to the value its adherents place upon it.

Perhaps it is necessary for people to leave the Outer Hebrides and live elsewhere in order to assess the advantages of island life against its disadvantages; but to attempt to create a life style as materially the same as that of the mainland seems to me to be self-defeating. A life that offers naturally fewer material rewards needs people committed to the benefits of that life in order to make it work. Every book about the 'Problems of the Crofting Communities' stops short at stating that many of the indigenous crofting community don't want to croft anymore, or are too old when they inherit their crofts to engage in the back-breaking labour necessary to get the land back into good heart. There is a lot of talk about 'rights' these days but the land has rights too, and to see it lying idle and wasted when someone somewhere would be prepared to work it is surely as wrong as when landlords maintained their sheep on good ground while landless men watched their children go hungry.

FOURTEEN

If any man be disposed to live a solitary, retired life,
and to withdraw from the noise of the world, he may
have a place of retreat there in a small island, or in the
corner of a large one where he may enjoy himself and
live at a very cheap rate.

Martin Martin

T̲HE QUIET LOW-COST LIFE THAT
Martin Martin advocated 300 years ago for those who wanted to be
out of the mainstream of the world's business is still as viable a proposition today as Janet and David Miles have demonstrated. The
'solitary, retired life' was not so apparent when I was there in the
summer, with the café operating and friends coming and going, but
that is only for about four months of the year. During the remaining
eight there are few diversions, except for the ubiquitous television,
and people have only themselves and their immediate family to rely
upon, especially when made house-bound by weeks of storm. Even
a couple with as good a relationship as Janet and David still require a
lot of personal inner strength and need to be very much in tune with
their surroundings in order to actively enjoy the isolation rather
than just to cope with it. Part of that being in tune with the place is
using the natural resources it offers and here necessity can well
prove a blessing. David and Janet had little choice but to live off
their small plot as far as was possible and the hours of work they
have to put into tending the soil has given them a much deeper
relationship with the island.

They have certainly proved the truth of Martin's assertion that
'there is nowhere in the known world where they may enjoy the
fruits of the land and the sea more cheaply.' I fared better at Scarista
Studio than I did during the whole of the rest of my stay and almost

everything we ate was either home-grown or free produce of the sea. We even had delicious fresh scallops the size of tea-plates one day, supplied by neighbours who had caught more than they required for themselves. Before the days of the deep freeze this sharing out of what was available was practised all the time, and self-sufficiency was on a community rather than a personal basis. Obviously this sort of life makes it difficult to have the whole of the world's produce available twelve months of the year as most town dwellers in the West have grown used to, but I'm not sure I enjoy this anyway. The pleasure of anticipation has been taken away from us to a large extent, and we don't look forward in the same way to the ripening of the various crops, and to eating things in their season. On the other hand some modern inventions do make a very positive contribution to this self-contained life style. The deep freeze for example is a greater asset to people like David and Janet who can now utilize all their excess produce than for people who fill it only with what they buy from shops.

We wanted mushrooms to cook with the scallops and went to pick them in the ancient sloping pastures above the roads. These are fields where some form of husbandry has been practised for at least four thousand years, though now they seem only barely in use. The heaps of lichened stone which lay about here and there in little hollows and against sheltered banks probably date back just as far, for they are the building material that has been used over and over again, in the construction of island peoples' dwellings. Early stone-age houses in these islands were built largely below the surface of the ground, for protection from the elements and the type persisted in places into recorded time. Written testimony lays claim to their having been dry and warm and some modern architects are again designing houses on this principle as being the most efficient for our climate. Much of the furnishings of those former island houses — beds, dressers, cupboards and shelves were ingeniously contrived from the same free standing, unmortared stone, and this too persisted in some places, well into the 17th century — though the only spot that I know of, where such things can still be seen is at the stone-age village of Skara Brae on Orkney, which was dramatically uncovered among sand dunes during a great storm.

As we searched for mushrooms, Janet named the wild flowers we came across and there were so many varieties that I wrote them down in my notebook so as to remember them. All of them were growing within the compass of a hundred yards or so and they read like a word picture of the fields — tormentil, scabious, bird's foot trefoil, sun-dew, self-heal, cow parsley, yellow rattle, hawk's bit, sheep's bit, red clover, white clover, buttercup, eyebright, bog asphodel, yellow vetch, poppy, St. John's wort, yarrow, cow parsley, sea campion, ladies bedstraw and most plentiful of all, wild thyme. It is a litany that conjures up not just the shape and colour of each small flower, but the island itself on one of its magical days of soft warmth; the sun shining and no wind but the gentlest of breezes to temper the heat and keep the midges away. A day when the scent of the flowers hangs heavy in the air and the colours of sea and sky have such depth and intensity, that every object is ringed with light.

It was not easy to leave Scarista and move on northwards, but summer was already well past its midway point and my time in the Outer Hebrides was fast running out. The morning I left was one of the loveliest of all. I walked down to the sea before breakfast, feeling still half asleep and wanting to wake myself up with a quick swim. As I came down over the dunes the sun broke through a gap in the thick grey cloud cover with such a sudden brightness that I was fully awake in the instant. It was an extraordinary light, very strong but diffused by the cloud — except where the sun had broken through in a few direct, bright shafts that made molten pools where they met the sea. A flock of high-flying gulls glowed where the rays caught them, like thin silver crescents against the dove-grey sky. The sea was jade-green and still and the sand was a glorious rich gold. Wild thyme had spread in a violet haze over the dunes, down to the margins of the beach, and the tall spiky marram grass waved above it. It was a scene that vibrated with a sort of primal joy, a stage set waiting for the play to begin. It remained like that for several minutes until further banks of cloud rolling in across the Atlantic changed it all entirely — as though floodlights had been abruptly turned off in a theatre.

*   *   *

No matter how sad I feel at parting from new friends or from places I would like to stay in longer, there is always a sense of freedom in setting off again that never palls. It makes little difference whether I'm in the middle of a desert, half way up a Himalayan mountain road or on a remote Hebridean island. The sense of not knowing what the day will bring, combined with being equipped with everything I need in order to be self-reliant quickens the blood with a feeling of adventure. I set off in sunshine around the west coast, along mile after mile of superb coastal scenery with here and there a huge standing stone, its roots deep in the flowers of the machair.

At the entrance to Borve Lodge a pair of buzzards were riding the wind above a stand of timber and I stopped to watch them. I find this one of the most dazzling displays in all nature and even Evans seems a poor tame thing compared with this exhibition of pure, unbridled freedom. The great, brown birds, little smaller than eagles soared and fell, twisted and turned and hung there motionless on the wind for nearly an hour, before vanishing to quarter the slopes of the hills beyond, hunting for rabbits and rodents. The coppice of tall trees above which they'd played is also a marvel, the only one in all of South Harris. I'm told that it was Lady Leverhume who planted the trees in the sheltered cleft of the hills. It would seem from her success that good quality timber could be re-introduced into the islands, at least in the more sheltered places. Unfortunately, the only tree people seem prepared to plant here nowadays is the depressing spruce, which yields quick profits as pulp for newsprint and ruins the ground it is grown in for a very long time afterwards.

The importance of Borve Lodge is its extensive and complicated series of trout lochs and the man responsible for managing them is Tony Scherr. He and his wife Heather live in the gate house where the front room has been turned into a craft shop selling all sorts of woollen goods and in pride of place, sporrans. It seemed a most unlikely thing for Sassenach incomers to be turning out so uniquely Scottish a commodity as sporrans, but once again a white settler had found a hole in the market and had set about learning how to fill it. It is eighteen years since the Scherrs came here, and Heather still remembers how bleak she found Harris when they rolled off the ferry after driving up non-stop, all the way from the South. They were a professional couple, living comfortably in their own home, with their children at school and Heather back at teaching. They came to Harris simply because Tony wanted the job. He had had a life-long passion for fish and this was his golden opportunity to spend his working time doing what he loved most, even though it meant a cut in material living standards. For Tony it was pure joy from the beginning and the children too had taken immediately to island life, but for Heather it was not nearly so simple and it had required quite a few years of adjustment before she arrived at the same level of contentment. From being a person with an independent life of her own she became overnight an over-worked house-wife, cooped up in a tiny cottage, coping under a welter of difficulties and missing her wider family back in England. Appetites increase enormously by the sea and Tony working hard outdoors was needing several square meals a day. It seemed she'd no sooner finished clearing up one meal than she was preparing the next and life had become an endless round of demands. The nearest shop was miles away and stocked pathetically little; the wind constantly blew the gas out on the stove and trying to provide dry clothes was a nightmare. Slowly as they improved their living conditions and Heather learnt to cope and adapt to the very different life style, she realised that she too had become addicted to island life and had no wish to return to the South.

The craft shop had filled the need for a creative outlet but had come about quite casually when her eldest daughter — then thirteen had wanted to make a little pocket money from selling the jewellery she'd been making out of polished stones and shells. They'd arranged them in the porch, suitably labelled and things had grown from there. Now the two eldest children are off her hands, Heather has found the time to attend courses for knitting and weaving, organised by the Development Board and she makes most of what she sells, including of course the sporrans. She was surprised to find that the courses had been only thinly patronised by the local people and that most of those who did attend dropped out before the end.

By the time I'd heard Heather's story, drunk a cup of coffee and admired her stock of goods, the day was well advanced and lack of sleep was catching up with me. I thought it would be a good idea to find a place to make camp soon and have a lazy ending to the day. The lovely Luskentyre beach was only a few miles further on so I decided to look for a place beside it. I'd already noticed on the map that there was a spit of sand dunes which appeared ideal for a quiet camp site. It was shaped like a huge rhinoceros horn protruding out into the sandy estuary from Seilibost. It was far from anywhere and at high tide was almost surrounded by sea; the only snag was that there appeared to be no fresh water nearby. I filled my container at a tap which was outside a school, closed for the summer and started off along the rough track leading to the spit. Dozens of rabbits scuttled from my path in startled surprise as I caught them unawares in my silent approach on Evans. They seemed to dart reproachful looks over their shoulders as they ran for the burrow entrances; remarkably plump rabbits who looked as though no-one disturbed them overmuch.

It was not until I was at the extreme tip of the peninsula that I found the ideal clearing among the rough hummocks of marram-bound dunes. It was like being on the prow of a tall ship, or in a light-house with the sea all around, except that I had a sweep of white beaches all around too with purple mountains edging three-quarters of the view. A patch of the small yellow flowers called appropriately, ladies bedstraw, had impacted the ground sufficiently for the tent pegs to hold as long as no gales blew. The small green nylon shape transformed the unfamiliar place at once into 'home' — a covered space of less than seven feet by three. With my stove, pans, lilo, sleeping bag and various other bits and pieces I made my small island of domesticity in the wilderness, just as Abraham and all other nomads had done before me. I didn't have my flocks of goats and camels about me of course, nor was my existence dependent upon finding water and grazing for them — had it been so it I would have been nicely placed since there was so much of both and to spare on Harris. I often remember our nomadic forebears when I'm sleeping in a tent instead of in a bed, and I must have fallen asleep thinking about them on this occasion because I dreamt about them setting up their camel skin tents in the Syrian desert and imagined I was there with them because I could hear the camels stamping about and getting in a state (as camels often do because of their being so highly strung), and I knew I had to get up and deal with them before they pulled out their tethering pegs and wandered off into the trackless wastes. When I surfaced properly I found that the short rest I'd planned had extended into several hours and it wasn't camels stamping about outside but a couple of young German campers looking for a place to put up their tent, having also noted the place from their maps.

The German couple had to make do with a place further back down the dunes but they joined me later for a cup of tea and an exchange of talk. The young man, Gunter was more interested in my equipment than in the view; he seemed to care very much that he had the best equipment that was available and asked the price of everything as though it was for sale. He seemed relieved that nothing I possessed, apart from the tent site could rival what he had. His girl friend sipped her tea and said very little; I formed the impression that he bullied her. Before I could settle down for the night I was obliged to return the visit and admire the German tent. It was not necessary to pretend, it was a distinctly superior set-up to mine with all sorts of refinements and comforts that must have been a great burden to carry about and would have been more appropriate to load on to the camels I'd dreamed of. I found I was right about him bullying his girl friend, so perhaps he also made her carry the bulk of the load.

The following day was warm with not a breath of wind and as soon as I put my head out, the midges descended in a cloud and I withdrew hurriedly to apply insect repellent to all exposed areas of skin. Midges are a menace before which the strongest quail. In America they call them 'no see ums' because they are so small. In Scotland you see them all too clearly, not because they are any larger, but because they move about in such vast numbers that they cover anything they settle upon in a grey cloud. They get every-where in seconds, under eyelids, into ears and nasal passages, and really the only way to cope with them is to be inside. I packed up camp hurriedly and got on my way, and in spite of the repellent I still collected several itchy bites. One way to escape the midges is to move faster than they can fly, and so I cycled on and on around Luskentyre Bay where the shallow sea flooding in over the sands was pale blue and green and only a very slightly different shade to the sky. The hills of the island of Taransay cast purple shadows over the water and the towering hills of North Harris formed a dark high wall to the north.

The road around the bay passes small hamlets and scattered houses and gets narrower and rougher until finally it comes to an end at a graveyard, beside what I finally decided was the most per-fect part of the huge bay. Here at the last isolated house, standing almost on the sea's edge I was invited in for a cup of tea by John Mac-Donald, an old bachelor living entirely alone since both his brothers had died within weeks of each other the previous year. He apolo-gised for the state of his house, saying it was 'just a bachelor's apart-ment'. It was an old-fashioned, strictly utilitarian interior and cer-tainly not fussily over-tidy. The very strong smell coming from a row of socks drying in front of the stove immediately assaulted my nose, made sensitive by days out of doors in the pure air. Apart from that it seemed very comfortable after my spartan tent and John's conversation as he plied me with strong tea and jam sandwiches, was interesting enough to take my mind entirely away from the socks.

'Yacket,' he said at the beginning of every phrase. 'Yacket, I was four years a shepherd on Pabbay, and three on Mingulay and Yacket, it was a lovely island Mingulay, a lovely island.' He'd been a shepherd for most of his long life, living quite alone on small islands and in remote glens. He had come back here to his parents' croft when they had grown too old to work it and his brothers had joined him later. The croft was not one that had been in the family for generations but had been awarded to them in the land settlements of the twenties; even so he moved about the place like a man who knows every rough step of it. I asked him what the shepherding life had been like and he said it had suited him very well; it was really just a matter of liking the sheep, he added. I was sure he had done that, I just couldn't imagine him throwing them around with the sort of callousness the film of the Shepherds of Berneray had displayed. He had three hundred sheep of his own to look after now, together with two cows, a couple of dogs and a scruffy but imperious white cat. One sheep was in the garden tethered up with a splint on its recently broken leg. The garden was a mess, with just a few sad potato plants growing in it, which the brown hens scratching around in the dirt hadn't managed to dig up yet. It all seemed far too much work for one man, especially one who was certainly well over seventy. But John MacDonald seemed perfectly happy and wore an air of great contentment and tranquillity, rare nowadays even in places like the Outer Hebrides. He wasn't the sort of man you felt sorry for, he just made you feel the richer for having spent some time with him.

The weather looked increasingly unpromising and it had grown so cold that I decided to take advantage of the hostel facilities at Stockinish. In any case I wanted to say hello to old acquaintances on the east coast and Stockinish was conveniently placed for that. The people at the Post Office recognised me at once, they had always been friendly to hostellers who congregated there most nights, waiting with a varied collection of containers for the cow to be milked. If the post mistress took to you and she wasn't inundated with young relations up from Glasgow, then you might be allowed to purchase fresh eggs too — real eggs laid by hens who had access to good, natural things like seaweed and grass, and produced eggs with yolks which were a lovely dark orange and had a taste instantly remembered from days before the appearance of the battery hen. But with eggs at a premium because so little other fresh food was available and hostellers avid for them, tracking down fresh sources of supply became quite a business. Once I called at a weaver's tin shed because hens were scratching away outside the door and I had a long conversation with the young man clattering away inside, after which I forgot about the eggs. The conversation was through the medium of a pencil and scraps of paper, as the young weaver was deaf and dumb. Many Harris houses have looms, mostly in a shed away from the house, for the noise they make is deafening. This young man wasn't bothered by the noise but nonetheless he hated weaving finding it mechanical and boring. What he wanted to do was to paint, and he waved his arms towards the walls of his shed which were covered with crude bright scenes executed in oils on hardboard. He wrote that he would dearly like to have lessons and just paint all day but when I asked him why he didn't he just shrugged hopelessly. Later I learnt that he had elderly parents who did not take his painting seriously and thought that weaving would provide a better future for him when they had gone. He was like a caged bird in that shed.

Stockinish hadn't changed I thought as I cycled down the last precipitous bend of the single-track road and saw it lying there below as always, a straggle of small buildings spread out along the shore of the thin thrusting finger of the loch, with rough fields of which no two were the same shape or size. There was still a cow to milk at the Post Office, but nothing to sell over the counter except stamps and a loaf of stale bread — there was a van but not today. The cottage next to the hostel still had its kitchen chairs outside the door, laden with knitted stockings, socks and sweaters to tempt the hostellers, and the red tin shed on the corner also displayed its handknits and rolls of hairy Harris tweed, with the same old sign grown a little dimmer and more rust specked: HARRIS TWEED SOLD HERE. The same two old men sat on the bench in front of it, giving a sideways tilt of the heads to the few passers by.

But when the first delight of remembered things was past I could see that there had been changes. Some smart modern fishing boats were now moored in the newly refurbished harbour and there was a novel air of prosperity about the seaward end of the village, with new and upgraded houses and lots of signs of activity. The landward end was shabbier and many of the small fields wore a look of neglect which was new since my last visit. In the croft behind the hostel, another source of eggs for hostellers, were a couple of men on holiday who were cutting the hay, though they wielded the long two-handled scythes as only islanders born to it can, in slow wide sweeps, unconsciously graceful. I photographed them at the task realising suddenly that I might never see it done again and when I told the men why I wanted a record of their work, they agreed that there could not be much future for this sort of crofting and that few of the younger men would know how to do it anyway.

The land along the coast from Stockinish up towards Tarbert is not so barren and rocky as the Bays area, but the fields are very small and will never be able to be worked by tractor. It is an area of fairy-tale beauty of which the narrow fields sloping down to the water's edge, dotted about with the stooks of hay are an essential element. Worked fields provide shades of light and texture that are entirely absent from land that reverts to its natural state. It hurts me deeply to imagine this intimate, domestic landscape totally derelict and covered in rushes and bracken like so many deserted places in the highlands and islands.

I waited out the inclement spell of weather at the hostel, though I slept in the tent as the place was so full. The difficulty of finding a small, flattish piece of ground that was not soggy, was almost insurmountable. I finished up with it pitched over the top of the newly laid drainage pipe and even then my head was considerably lower than my feet. Some young hostellers, who had abandoned their tents for a hostel bed made my stay much more comfortable by lending me an extra mat and pillow and also provided some really good midge repellant. The crowd at the hostel was as usual from a wide variety of countries — America, Japan, Europe and even England, most of them 'first-timers' and all of them were entranced with the Outer Hebrides in spite of the weather. Two middle-aged West Coast Americans stated firmly that they would have been disappointed if there had been no rain, since that was what they had expected and had come prepared for. Sunshine they had gotten in plenty back home. No-one else was quite that philosophical, though most agreed that Hebridean rain had a soft attractive quality as long as it didn't go on too long. There were two girls from Holland whom I liked particularly and we agreed to meet up again later at Stornoway where we would all be taking the boat back to the mainland.

Before I left Harris, I was determined to visit a weaver whom I had heard a great deal about over the years. Her name was Marion Campbell and many articles had been written about her work and methods. I had also met several young American girls who had spent whole summers on Harris in order to study her techniques and they had waxed lyrical about her work, character, life-style and so forth unti I thought Harris must be harbouring its own latter day version of William Morris. So when I set off along the switchback road to Plocrapool one morning I was expecting someone very special indeed. I found the house perched superbly on a ridge between a large island-studded inland loch and an island-studded bay. It was an ordinary unpretentious Hebridean cottage with little concession to comfort and none at all to style or decoration. Not that it needed much of the last two with a view like that across Scalpay and the Shiant Islands to the hazy hills of Skye.

Some Americans were there before me and I was ushered in to join them. Marion Campbell was an upright island woman with white hair and rosy cheeks and certainly she didn't look anything like the 75 years she claimed. The American couple were treating her with great deference, as though she was royalty and she seemed not unpleased by this. They were buying a length of rather bright soft green tweed and thanking her profusely for selling it to them. Turning to me she said that if I'd come to buy tweed there was none at all, it was all sold before ever it was warped up. I was glad of that since I was not wanting any, and in any case I preferred a closer woven, heavier type.

Once the Americans had gone I was treated to what was obviously a well practised talk on the weaver's art and shown her scrapbook with all her press cuttings. I'm not surprised that she had become famous, for even among a nation of 'characters' she was outstanding and had moreover the ability to communicate her enthusiasm. To me she came over as a pure work-aholic who had discovered weaving at the age of twelve and had been addicted to it ever since. Her single-mindedness reminded me more of an incomer than of an island woman.

I had expected that all her dyes would be extracted from natural sources like seaweed and rushes and was disappointed when she said they were all powders except for crotal, which is the lichen that grows on rocks and gives the warm brown background shade to Harris tweed. Her weaving shed was full of holes, and cold even in mid-summer. How she manages the chills and winds of winter there defied my imagination. Her loom was an old-fashioned wooden one, a type that has been largely replaced now and I think it is this loom which is responsible for the looser weave she produces. Demonstrating its use, she seemed to take on a different quality altogether, softer, loving almost — like a mother with a young child. The very repetition of the movements seemed to afford her great pleasure and I think she became quite unaware of my presence and could have gone on throwing the bobbin across into eternity. She was the antithesis of the deaf mute boy at Stockinish; what was for him a prison was her refuge.

F I F T E E N

In this countrie of Harray north-wart, betwixt it and
the Leozus are mony forests, mony deer.

Dean Munro

…and there is none permitted to hunt there without
a licence, from the steward to the forester.

Martin Martin

To the north of the west loch
Tarbert, above the narrow waist of Harris, a great line of barren hills
juts out westwards into the Atlantic. This is the deer forest of North
Harris, which forms the barrier to the flatter lands of Lewis beyond.
I doubt there is even a bush of any size growing in these 'forests' but
enough tough herbage finds a foothold there to nourish the herds of
red deer who have roamed the hills since they retreated upwards
from the more fertile lower glens at the coming of man. Innumerable small burns drain the area, joining together to form rivers
which plunge in rocky falls down the steep slopes towards the sea.

To these rivers come the Atlantic salmon after their epic journeys from the Arctic seas. They run the falls in a series of spectacular
leaps, battling against the water rushing down over the slippery
rocks; taking advantage of any pocket of weaker flow which offers
them a temporary respite. Every inch of the salmon in their thrilling
up-stream passage portrays a pure concentration of power and purpose. Onwards and upwards they travel against all seeming reason
and probability, fighting every inch of the way; falling back again and
again, but always persisting until eventually they reach the head
waters of the small upland burn where they were spawned some
years before and where they in turn will spawn another generation
before heading back out to the open sea. I had never witnessed this
annual miracle except on film, always having been where it happens
either too late or too early. This year I was out long enough not to

miss it and this was why I was bound for a place called Amhuinn-suidhe, half way along the line of the North Harris hills, where the salmon are said to run more plentifully than anywhere else in the Outer Hebrides.

The narrow road to Amhuinnsuidhe (pronounced Armin-suey) runs along the foot of the towering mass, around the northern shores of West Loch Tarbert and there is no part of that road that is not going either steeply up or down. I had with me enough provisions for several days, so Evans was well-laden and as it was raining copiously I was wearing my constricting waterproofs, circumstances that do not add to the ease of cycling. No landscape is really improved by thin grey rain with no hint of sunshine behind the clouds and this was such a day; altogether one to be borne rather than enjoyed. Shortly after leaving the Stornoway road the ugly shell of a gaunt building appeared, which had once been the heart of a Norwegian whaling station, built early this century and abandoned long since. After that there was only a school, miles from anywhere and about twenty scattered houses, until the castle of Amhuinn-suidhe appeared fourteen miles further on.

Somewhere along this road my purse fell from my pocket and the first I knew of it was when I was hailed from a car, the driver of which had passed me going in the other direction an hour before. Since there was no other person on the road he had surmised that the purse must be mine and had kindly turned his car around and pursued me with it. It was a purse in which I carried all things monetary, including my bank and credit cards and it was nice to get it back before I'd even realised that I'd lost it. What I didn't know at the time was that the cards had parted company with the purse and were at that moment travelling around in a car with some German visitors who were determined to hand them over personally or else take them back to Germany as a souvenir. I wasted a lot of time over the next two days finding a telephone and ringing the local police and my bank in London to inform them of my loss. In the meantime I kept coming across the trail of the cards, as people reported having been stopped and aked if they were Selby, but in spite of having a description of the car and occupants the police (very keen to help) didn't succeed in finding them; nor did it occur to the Germans to deposit the cards at a police station. Finally they enquired for a Selby at the Harris Hotel, Tarbert just before they caught the ferry to Skye and the manager had the sense to explain that they must leave the cards with him rather than taking them off the island.

I arrived at Amhuinnsuidhe unaware as yet of my loss, wet and wind-buffetted and hoping to find the shelter of a more substantial roof than the tent. After all the miles of rough, rain-soaked moorland it was rather strange to cycle through the well-kept grounds of a stately mansion, close enough to peer in through the ground floor windows. It must be frightfully galling to own all those acres and have a public road passing just in front of your doorstep. There has always been a stately pile somewhere in the area — Dean Munro notes that the MacLeod hunted here and that traditionally one particular hill was always reserved for his exclusive use. The present 'castle' dates from 1864 when Lord Dunmore had it built in the popular Victorian Scottish baronial style — all turrets and castellations. James Barrie is said to have written his play Mary Rose here, inspired by the aura of Hebridean mystery and legend. The present owner is an incomer but not a white settler, for he is Swiss and if he is settled anywhere it is probably in his own well-regulated country. He spends just a week or so here each year and further weeks on his other Scottish estates. I was told that when he visits this castle he likes to walk around with his housekeeper asking what parts of the surrounding hills belong to him.

For the rest of the year Amhuinnsuidhe is let by the week at a suitably high rent to sporting persons. It was Norfolk butchers who had it while I was there, trying their hand at killing salmon for a change and having to be discouraged (some of them at least) from taking them in too facile a manner from the lower pools, where the salmon are building up strength for their run. The butchers were having a fine week for the salmon were coming in thick and fast and on the evenings I spent watching them leaping the first of the falls it seemed as though the water boiled with their progress.

I didn't get to see the extensively refurbished interior of the castle as I was visiting 'below stairs' which came about as a result of another rumour of the missing cards. The Harris Hotel had thought Selby might be one of the castle's sporting types and had telephoned to enquire and so when I appeared I was invited in to use the telephone. It was a fascinating turn about from traditional notions of above and below stairs. The arbiters and protectors of good taste and custom were certainly those on the lower floors who acted as cooks, maids and gamekeepers, waiting upon those lodged above whose accents and manners had been far less expensively nurtured. The paying guests seemed determined to get value for money and nothing at all was sent back from table and 'more gravy' was demanded at frequent intervals. A pity this, as the dinner I had been invited to share depended upon the plates not being scraped quite clean. Some of these same guests damned themselves further in my eyes the following day by sounding the horns of their flashy motor cars just behind me on the single-track road when they wanted to pass in quite impossible places on uphill bends.

A few of the staff were incipient white settlers. They were there because the job provided a means for them to stay where they most wanted to be, and from where they could more easily seek a place of their own. Others had a taste for the sporting life themselves and were in the ideal position to indulge this passion with superlative fishing and stalking. One such was the head ghillie, a young man who reminded me of the handsome Seth in Cold Comfort Farm. In his skin tight knee breeches, with shirt casually open to the waist he trailed his blonde good looks around the enormous flag-stoned kitchen, striking poses, like a caricature of all the caddish game-keepers who ever sent young scullery maids all of a quiver.

At the bottom of the pecking order were the watchers who had the rotten job of staying out all night, roaming the hills and the river banks in order to deter or catch poachers. It must be a great tempta-tion to seek shelter on wild blustery nights, like the one I experi-enced there and two of the watchers did succumb because when I awoke at two in the morning in my B&B at the Post Office, it was because of the roars of laughter and merry conversation coming from the adjacent bedroom. When I mentioned the incident the fol-lowing morning the post mistress said it was just the river watchers who'd come in for a cup of tea and hadn't wanted to go back out into the wet cold night. Martin Martin writes that in former times when the steward caught watchmen napping 'he stript them of their clothes and deferred their personal punishments to the proprietor of the place' — this would hardly be fair at Amhuinnsuidhe, for they could freeze to death while waiting for their absentee landlord.

In temporary business quarters above the unused castle stables I found another white settler with a flair for finding an unfilled niche. She'd wandered about the world a little before losing her heart to Amhuinnshuidhe and having done so stuck out for settling there. It. had to be this very spot she said which made for difficulties since there was no sort of accommodation available. After sticking it out in her tent for a while the Post Office had come to her aid, renting her the minute caravan tucked into a corner of their garden. Susan had already worked out her means of livelihood — with all that tweed about there was no-one making it up in modern styles to individual requirements, and with some background in sewing and design she thought she could do that. She started with difficulty, making things in the caravan. The floor space was a couple of inches wider than the tweed so it was not actually impossible to cut out the garments. Now, under the name of Suza she is in seventh heaven in her spacious loft, turning out comfortable attractive clothing, far removed from traditional stiffly tailored tweed costumes.

The road continues round the wild coast beyond Amhuinn-suidhe to end at Hushinish Point and the jetty which once served the islanders of Scarp. Here Janet Miles had spent her summer painting and become captivated by island scenery. I rode there on a day when the blustery wind was still bending the scurries of sharp-pointed rain into an horizontal onslaught. I took shelter in a shed on the jetty, where through the open door I could see across the white-capped waves of the narrow sound to Scarp. There were houses dotted about all over the landward-facing slopes; from this distance they appeared still habitable and the fields wore no apparent look of abandonment. It appeared far more poignant, shocking even, than abandoned islands where nature had softened the scene, moving in and blurring the outlines. This was a place not of history but of our time. Some of the houses were holiday homes now and I had even heard of a grandiose development scheme for making the whole island into a super luxury hotel complex. None of that seemed in the least relevant to the tragedy the scene depicted. It was almost incomprehensible that something so long in the making had just ceased — a whole unique community destroyed and scattered, not through plague, war, famine or any tangible catastrophe but simply because it wasn't worth the effort anymore. The life it stood for no longer had the value to compete with modern expectations.

I stayed there for a long time walking around the coast which was totally deserted and very beautiful with high cliffs and a few sandy coves at their feet. I was glad I'd lingered because after I'd returned and cooked lunch in the shelter of the hut I met a native of the place, who having left Harris for a better life had chosen to return. I found this a comforting encounter while contemplating deserted Scarp. He had become a successful accountant in England but it had seemed to him that the quality of life, particularly for his family was nowhere near what they could enjoy back home on Harris. It was lobster fishing he was returning to in a small village just short of Hushinish Point. He didn't think he'd make half the money he'd been used to in the city, and he certainly wouldn't have the sort of security he'd enjoyed there but he knew he was doing the right thing, especially for his children.

When I thought about our conversation later I realised he had not spelled out what those 'qualities of life' were, other than in concrete terms of space and safety etc. The underlying reasons that draw a person back to a place like Harris are perhaps not possible to put into words and must always be more implied than stated. But there can be no doubt of the profound effect upon the other members of a small community of having a young man returning from choice to their way of life. For the former inhabitants of Scarp such a return is no longer possible for its social structures are dismantled and destroyed and it would have to be incomers starting from scratch who chose to build a new way of life there. I wondered if it was such new beginnings that had earned the Outer Hebrides their name of Islands of Strangers.

Once I'd collected my credit cards from the Harris Hotel and tucked them away more securely, there was nothing further to prevent me from climbing up the saddle of the North Harris hills and crossing over into Lewis or 'The Leozus' as the Dean has it. After all the strong southerly winds of the past few days it turned northerly and blew cold rain into my face for most of the morning, making hard work of the ride. The rain obscured all the hills so there was nothing but water-logged peat to be seen. I've never ridden along the eastern side of Lewis without longing to reach Stornoway as soon as possible. Perhaps I haven't seen it at its best, but after coming from the diverse scenery of Harris, the road to Stornoway seems to go unendingly across a dreary boggy moor.

Stornoway is thriving, every time I see it, its suburbs having spread out a little further. The newcomers have mostly come in from the countryside and in this respect the place is reminiscent of Istanbul, Mexico City or Buenos Aires except that everyone seems decently housed and relatively prosperous. There are more shops selling a wider selection of goods especially alcohol, there is even one devoted entirely to hats. Construction yards for the oil industry has re-established some of the town's 18th and 19th century prosperity when it flourished on kelp and fish.

A Pakistani community of shopkeepers settled in Stornoway many years ago and is now producing its third generation of babies. I met one young Pakistani mother when I spotted a large jar of Bombay Mix in her father's shop window and went in to buy some. She had a small daughter at her knee and was expecting another baby soon; she spoke with a charming island accent but claimed that her Gaelic was not up to her husband's standard and he had been here only a few years. Like many Asian girls she had been sent to Pakistan as a teenager in order to make a suitable match. She much preferred life in the Outer Hebrides she told me and wouldn't want to live in Pakistan. Having witnessed the restricted life the average woman in Pakistan leads, I am not surprised. The oldest and most prestigious shop is also owned by a Pakistani white settler of long standing. He has kept the name — James Mackenzie and it is still possible to buy a wide range of goods, from a dustbin to a reproduction of Stag at Bay there. But there are subtle indications that it is not a native establishment — there is a flavour of the subcontinent about many of the ornaments and a notice which reads 'Shoplifting is harmful to the reputation and injurious to the pocket' reminded me at once of similarly phrased notices on the roads of the Himalayan passes.

I went straight to the Y.M.C.A. to meet the Dutch girls, Lilian and Jose as arranged. They were not there but there was a note informing me that the dirt in the place had defeated them and they were camping instead and had reserved a place for me. As I came out pursued by the cries of drunken youths, carving up a couple of snooker tables, I met the two Canadian cyclists I had first seen on North Uist. 'You're not thinking of staying there?' they asked solicitously. 'No, my friends say it's too dirty,' I replied. 'Dirty, hell,' they said. 'It's not the dirt that's the worry it's the damn punks.' It transpired that they'd stayed there the previous night and had been warned by the person in charge to barricade their door. They did so, but it hadn't stood up to having a human battering ram being continually thrown at it. After it had been broken down, they'd been entertained to a little blood letting amongst the young interlopers — it seemed they had wanted an audience. It was all pure showing off the Canadians claimed and they were only 'soft punks, not real hard cases' but even so the Canadians had felt rather threatened and at 2 a.m. in the rain they had cleared out and bivouacked among the rhododendron bushes in the adjacent park. They were currently trying to dry out their gear. When I met up with Lilian and Jose they confirmed that there had been rather a lot of blood about and they'd assumed someone had cut their thumb or something.

After I'd pitched my tent, we all three dined in a bar in town, still pursuing the subject of the Y.M.C.A. punks on Lewis seemed ridiculous to me but a family man dining in the same bar with his wife joined in our conversation and said that 'Life on the Islands was getting stupid.' There was too much of everything — too much time and too much money and the young didn't know what to do with it all. Another war or national service was needed to sort them out. Jose, who'd been sitting in Scottish fields for the last year, watching sheep as part of her Ph.D on animal behaviour, and heartily wishing she'd chosen some other animal to study, didn't agree at all. She said she thought the weather had a lot to do with it and that even the sheep were affected by all this rain and could become hyper-aggressive when it continued for too long. That rather finished the conversation as the man clearly wasn't sure if Jose was joking or deranged. We went back and finished up the remains of an excellent malt whisky and I slept well in spite of continuous rain drumming on the nylon, inches from my head.

While we were packing our tents the following morning with the unrelenting rain still falling, a man put his head out of a caravan door and invited us in for a cup of tea. He had an amazing Aberdonian accent, which was quite incomprehensible to Jose and Lilian and almost so to me. We had to take off our shoes before we came into the van in case we muddied the carpet. He'd just rented it the night before on a long let and wanted confirmation that he had a bargain. We were taken on a tour in our socks.

'Full length bath, never had that before. Fridge too, and it works. And will you look here, two separate bedrooms and no beds in the sitting room. Would you believe it for £30 a week? It should by £50 by rights but he's let me have it cheap because I'll be here for a bit.'

I asked him why he was here and he said it was for business and when I asked what that was he said vaguely, 'Oh fixing things, organising.' He was extremely evasive about everything except the low-priced fascinations of his caravan's amenities. We left as soon as we decently could, Jose and Lilian to catch the ferry and me to head off in the rain for the Butt of Lewis.

Evans badly needed more oil and made heavy weather of the climb up the Glen Mhor Barvas to the west coast. I was shocked to see how rusty he'd become in the weeks we'd been out here — sea air and incessant rain play havoc with machinery. At Barvas I found a garage and a friendly mechanic who applied quantities of oil to the chain and the block. After which I turned north and with the wind behind me and the pedals turning more easily I proceeded at a livelier pace towards the northern tip of the Long Island. I can't say that I found any of the way beautiful and the further I went the bleaker it became. Above the village of Ballantrushal the tallest standing stone in the Outer Hebrides — Clach an Trushal, overlooked the sea and road, like an admonishing finger warning off strangers.

The closer I got to the end of the land, the denser the habitations appeared to be, though this was only in comparison with greater areas of nothingness. Houses straggled along cheek by jowl beside the continuous ribbon of the road, with sour looking fields running down to the coast behind them. Although I knew that depopulation was as acute here as anywhere it wasn't apparent except in the unworked fields. The openness of the landscape was daunting, like a prairie, there seemed nowhere at all to hide from prying eyes or from the elements — no wonder, I thought, that earlier settlers had built their houses half underground. Near the final, most northerly village of Europie was the tiny 12th century chapel of St. Moluag in the middle of flat, watery fields. One of the three original centres for Christianising the islands, it isn't used now or visited much, and although I found it well restored there seemed no atmosphere about it. It just sat there in the fields unconnected with anything.

The lands ends with a series of slabs sliced off by the sea over the millennia. Narrow channels of water swirl and boil up around the feet of these island stacks which are near enough almost to leap across. The temptation to try such a leap made me shake with fear and move back from the edge. The Butt of Lewis Lighthouse almost at my elbow, sounds out a harsh repeated note of implacable warning into the surrounding mist and gulls shriek back at it derisively. From just around the corner in the small, pretty port of Sto men of this parish used once to set out to collect the annual rents from the tiny island of North Rona — a mere dot in the ocean, more isolated even than St. Kilda. It supported only five families, an ancient people who took their surnames from the colours of the sky and the rainbow. When they were last visited in the 16th century they still practised the 'old religion' and performed a circle 'sunwise' around their visitors to honour them. They skinned their sheep whole and stuffed the skins with barley meal as a gift — a princely gift from so small and wild a place. An ecclesiastic with more condemnation than wonder in his heart left a last account of these people of North Rona. When the Lewis men next came they found a young woman with a baby at her breast, both dead upon the cliffs and investigating further they discovered that all the folk had perished of starvation. It seems that seamen from a passing ship had come ashore and stolen the island bull and possibly other livestock too, and rats from another ship had swum ashore and devoured all the store of grain. North Rona is now the main breeding ground of the grey Atlantic seal and I would dearly love to visit it, though so far I have discovered no way of doing so.

I had passed an inn on the way to the Butt of Lewis and decided to take a room there for the night. Although the rain had stopped and the skies were already turning into a spectacular canvas which made me realise where the beauty of the place really lay, still I had no wish to put up the tent. The daunting openness of the landscape, further enhanced by these increasingly enormous skies made me yearn for more substantial walls, behind which I could escape from nature for while. The desire to be warm and cosy seemed suddenly of primary importance.

My disappointment at finding the inn full was all the keener for having anticipated so longingly all the small delights of indoor life — like china plates and whisky in a glass, a fireside and a soft bed with sheets and blankets. 'You'll find nowhere else around here,' said the landlady, with what I could not help thinking was a degree of satisfaction. 'No it will be Stornoway that's your nearest.' So there was nothing for it but the tent and I began to look for a suitable pitch. This proved surprisingly difficult; what land was not in cultivation, or at least fenced was totally unsuitable in one way or another. I spent an hour going down track after track only to withdraw and try somewhere else. Then I remembered that I had been given an introduction to some people living in a manse in the area and I decided to call and see what they could suggest. I found the place with no difficulty, all on its own at the end of a track. It was a nicely-proportioned, long stone house with a small walled garden alongside and some out-buildings — a small oasis of cultivated neatness in the generally disordered surroundings. No-one answered my knock on the door however and the only living creatures around were three or four friendly cats.

It was the time for executive decisions. Clearly I could not cycle back to Stornoway; there seemed no place else to pitch a tent and I suspected more foul weather before morning. If it was my pretty walled garden I asked myself, with a green and tempting lawn in the middle, would I mind a traveller in need pitching her tent in its shelter? Of course I wouldn't, and from what I had heard of the Vaughans who lived here they would not mind either. Having made my decision I wrote a note to pin to the front door, explaining that there was an elderly female cyclist (I was feeling rather ancient by this time) camping in their garden and how I hoped they wouldn't mind. After which I erected the tent and crawled into it, just in time to avoid another inundation.

The good thing about a very small tent is that you can warm it up in no time with the aid of a candle — as long as you don't set fire to the walls that is and have altogether too much heat. So when I'd lit my stub of candle and managed to wriggle out of my wet clothes and had had a little whisky from a plastic mug, life seemed altogether more acceptable. I cooked supper in a spirit of contentment and dropped off to sleep soon afterwards to the sound of strong winds held at bay behind the garden walls and rain lashing down in sudden brief scurries on the taut nylon of my snug little shelter. I thought I heard voices and saw some flashing lights at some period in the night but exhausted with the cycling and the weather I merely turned over and slept more soundly. I think there are few places in the world where I would feel the degree of trust necessary to be able to do that.

When I crawled out the following morning it was to a larkspur-coloured sky with high plumed wind-clouds stretched across it. In one of the windows of the house, I saw a large notice which read 'Welcome, come and have breakfast' so I went in and met another fascinating family of white settlers, Dai and Jenny Vaughan who had moved up here with their two young children twelve years ago. It was not in their case an addiction to the Outer Hebrides but a need for a large house that initially brought them here and life has not been without friction for them in this bastion of strict Presbyterianism. It isn't strange that it was a manse that they found since few houses in the islands were ever of any size except for the establishments of the lairds and the gentlemen of the cloth.

The manse was built in the early years of the 19th century, by Thomas Telford who was responsible for many of the island roads and churches, as well as being employed to do coastal surveys and write economic reports etc., for in his day it was still the fashion for energetic and able people to operate on a much wider front and not be confined to ever narrower spheres of specialisation as is the case today. Following the Disruption of 1843, church and manse became the objects of open contention between the Established Church and the Free Church, both claiming their sole right to the 'House of God'. The government of the day had a battleship off-shore, its guns trained upon the church ready to reduce it to rubble should the violent feelings of the two parties erupt into bloodshed. With only an estimated 500 of the 20,000 inhabitants of Lewis still adhering to the Established Church it was not long before the church building was dismantled and built elsewhere, leaving the manse to slowly moulder around a succession of flockless ecclesiastics.

Jenny and David have restored the place simply and effectively, creating a large open space which makes the most of the light. They are both artists and have worked together for years on *trompe-l'oeil* interiors in nightclubs and private houses. I haven't seen this work myself, only reproductions, but from their folio, it appears masterly and exciting, full of the invention and illusions of that genre. They were currently finishing off a commissioned painting of a cricket match. A very green English picture seen through an open window at the height of summer, intensely detailed so that it was impossible to take it all in at once and every time the eye returned to it there was something that had been missed before. They painted on it together at the same time, changing sides occasionally for a new perspective.

Of all the white settlers I met, I thought David and Jenny were the toughest and they needed to be in order to survive in Ness. David's background could not really be more at odds with those of his neighbours, being non-conformist in the truest sense. He had been educated at Ampleforth College and had gone straight from there to painting scenery in the theatre. A term at the Architects Association had bored him by its slow pace and rigidity, and he had returned to painting scenery. After a period of travel he had gone to Cornwall to paint and there he had met Jenny who had already established her painting life. With the birth of their children they had to adapt somewhat and create a permanent home. It was Jenny's mother who heard of the manse at Ness and when they went to look at it, David had one of those strange *déjà vu* experiences as soon as he walked inside. After that they had to have it, and like George Jackson on North Uist, they had had to outbid some Americans for the privilege.

They live as self-sufficient a life as possible, but David says for them 'Self-sufficiency doesn't come cheap,' adding, 'but we do have space.' They have obviously worked tremendously hard on the house and the garden. They gave up painting *trompe-l'oeil* interiors for a while and started to design high-fashion crochet and knitwear, using local people to make up their designs. This became too successful for their way of life and for island efficiency, as the demands of fashion houses in New York and London far outstripped supply.

All in all it seemed better for the children to attend boarding school in England and for Dai and Jenny to take on further commissions for interiors during term times. This was their current mode of life while they pondered possible alternatives.

Organising local dances was another of David's earlier ventures and here he ran foul of the Free Church who strongly disapproved of dances and powerful as that body is in Lewis it was bound to win in the end. Late one night the house was raided by two separate posses of policeman suddenly charging in through both entrances. Since they failed to find anything — David assumes they were looking for drugs, they simply put a tail on him everywhere he went and eventually they got him for alleged drunken driving. After that the Ness Hall was denied him and there have been no dances held there since. It is in this parish that the cinema manager was cursed for showing *Jesus Christ Super Star* and where the cinema was subsequently closed for alleged breaches of safety regulations. It was also to this parish that the Reverend Angus Smith was sent after his victory in preventing the Sunday ferry operating on Skye. I heard a story here which although I cannot vouch for its veracity does admirably sum up the attitude of the Free Church. An Anglican minister who was holidaying on Lewis was caught walking after morning service by a local Free Church elder and was reprimanded by him for so doing. The Minister replied that even Our Lord had taken a walk on the Sabbath and quoted a chapter and verse including the line 'the Sabbath was made for man, not man for the Sabbath.' To which the elder had made the memorable rejoinder, 'Aye well He might have got away with such goings on there in those times but He'd no get away with it here!'

After a day or so with the Vaughans I began to appreciate the less immediately obvious natural charms of Ness, but even so I doubt I could ever be persuaded to settle there. It must take as strong a relationship as the Vaughans appear to have even to make the attempt, for they seem like an island isolated within an island and the thought that they have survived here for twelve years fills me with the deepest respect for them.

SIXTEEN

On the south side of the island of Bernera there are
small islands without the entrance, which contribute
much to the security of the harbour, by breaking the
wind and the sea which come from the great ocean.

Martin Martin

ON THE WEST COAST OF LEWIS,
about thirty miles south of the Butt is a very large bay called Loch
Roag. This must have been the religious focus of all the Outer
Hebrides in the Stone Age, for here were erected the greatest monuments of that time. The colonnaded stone circle of Callanish with its
unique cruciform shape is second in importance only to Stonehenge. Many other smaller circles in the area, within a radius of ten
miles or so are also still intact and are apparently connected in some
way with the Callanish circle, possibly to aid astronomical observations and predictions. There is also a splendid broch nearby — a circular, double-skinned tower, built of huge slabs of undressed stone,
enclosing an open space at the centre. It was in such buildings that
Celtic tribes took shelter in times of danger, safely lodged within the
hollow walls, with their livestock secure in the middle area. The
island-studded bay is a place of great beauty protected by shapely
hills and as Martin points out it is also well sheltered from the
weather 'which comes from the great ocean'.

In the centre of the loch is the island of Great Bernera, and it was
here at its extreme seaward point, in a small sandy cove that I set up
my camp, overlooking Little Bernera, Flodday and Gallan Head
(where once whales were to be seen in such large numbers that the
Gallan Whale was thought to be a distinct species). The people of
Great Bernera had fought hard to gain possession of their island in

the land wars, insisting that the farm which occupied much of the best land be divided up into crofts and given to the landless cottars, for as they wrote to the Board '... There are 43 souls of us and surely our lives are of more account than one man and his sheep,' and they occupied the land forthwith until they were forcibly ejected and bound over to keep the peace. In more recent times the people of Great Bernera again threatened to take matters into their own hands; this time their demand was for a bridge over the narrow sound which separates them from Lewis. As the authorities delayed and prevaricated, the men threatened to blow up the landward facing cliffs and create a causeway for themselves — the bridge was built before they could put their threat into effect and they are reputedly doing very well with the lobster fishing at present.

After I had spent some days wandering around the island and the adjacent coast, I spent a long day with the proprietor, a day that was endlessly fascinating and frustrating by turn. The Comte de Mirrilees, once Rouge Dragon Pursuivant and chief herald at the Queen's wedding had purchased Great Bernera twenty years before he had set foot upon it, having seen its impending sale advertised in a newspaper. At the time, he told me, he was busy with his other establishments — a *schloss* in Austria, a castle in the Pyrenees, another in Banff and houses in London, Paris, Le Touquet and Geneva; but the idea of an island had a certain romantic appeal which these other places lacked. Five years ago Robin Mirrilees had begun to think about his island when a small crofter's cottage had become vacant and he had bought it and moved in to take up his seigneurial role. He had had the little house done out in plastic imitation wood panelling and grandly named The Lodge. It had been left with about as much character as a hamburger bar and seemed a far cry from the grandeurs of the palatial residences he'd told me about. Only the personal momentos lying tastefully around on occasional tables and whatnots gave a flavour of his other life, so at odds with this rough, remote little island. Silver framed photographs and leather bound albums showed him at various stages of his life as herald, army officer and socialite, looking never less than extremely handsome whichever profile was presented to the camera.

He is busy now getting himself known as the 'Count of Great Bernera' and thinking up schemes to improve the economy of the island. I got the impression that while the locals watch him with a certain amount of wariness — landlords have never been popular figures out here, they also feel an amused tolerance, or even an affectionate respect for him as a 'character'. Several people told me about him over cups of tea and I was several times shown the local paper full of photographs of 'The Royals' visiting Great Bernera, with 'The Count' very much in evidence, dressed in Highland regalia. I though he had aspirations of being a present day Lord Leverhume, an idea not unpleasing to him, though he says he would go more slowly, winning the people's co-operation first. He has made a start with a small salmon farm and there are other dreams — a factory, an hotel and a football pitch — nothing really on the scale of his predecessor but plenty to keep a rather lonely man actively engaged in life.

His anecdotes were so amusing and provocative that only the pangs of hunger told me I had missed at least two of my normal meals. The Count didn't eat, he said, on the days when the local lady who attended to his needs was otherwise engaged, and he was very proud of his inability to be able to do anything culinary. I didn't feel able to tell him that I was slowly sinking from lack of food, and every time I tried to leave to set up my camp stove somewhere, another fascinating topic would be broached and I would be unable to extricate myself. Then he remembered that he had asked some French people to tea and begged me to stay and help entertain them, by which he meant get the tea ready, and such was his persuasive charm that I found myself submissively playing the part of kitchen maid while he rushed off to the nearest telephone to order cakes from the island shop.

The visitors, who had a holiday home on the island arrived soon after the Count had gone and while I was still digging around in the unfamiliar kitchen trying to find the necessaries for a polite tea party. As luck would have it, the visitors knew no English, so I had the additional task of making stilted conversation until Robin returned to take over in French that appeared as flawless and was certainly as voluble as his English. The tea party went on for four hours and as I was quite extraneous to the gathering with my inadequate grip on the French language, I would have left after doing the honours with the teapot, had not another visitor arrived.

This was a local archaeologist named Margaret Ponting, whom Don the American student had enthused about on South Uist. Another white settler captivated by the Outer Hebrides, she was largely self-taught but had made significant contributions to the knowledge of early Hebridean settlers, and was totally immersed in the prehistory of these islands. She was calling on the Count by appointment, in her official capacity as custodian of certain antiquities and seemed perturbed at finding other people present and became increasingly frustrated waiting for the French to depart. The Count had it seemed been responsible for seriously disturbing an important megalithic site on Great Bernera, for in the course of some work, one of a group of standing stones had been removed and he had had it put back the wrong way round. Margaret Ponting wasn't convinced that he was in the least repentant about the affair though I thought he seemed very nervous of her and was trying to hide from the wrath to come by prolonging the tea. Eventually however the French couple departed and Margaret Ponting had her chance. She had explained it all to me already while the waves of fluent French passed over our less polished heads. Now she tried hard to explain to the Count that it wasn't just a matter of restoring the site to its former state; valuable archaeological evidence had already been irreparably destroyed and further damage would occur if he went at it again without expert supervision. The Count for all his exercise of a charming urbanity still seemed quite unrepentant and Margaret Ponting even with the passionate single-mindedness of the truly committed was not going to succeed in making him see that scholarship was more important than his proprietorial rights.

Thinking that I could do nothing at all to help and conscious of my, by now, quite desperate hunger I asked the Count if he would mind me unpacking my food supplies in his kitchen and getting myself something to eat. Seeing his look of wistfulness, I added that I would fix him something too if he wished, an offer he jumped at. This made Margaret Ponting remember that she too hadn't eaten since daybreak, so the strained conversation was discontinued and we all retired to the kitchen, where after inspecting the refrigerator and pooling resources, I made the three of us soup and scrambled eggs and bacon, while Margaret Ponting cut bread and laid the table and the Count opened some bottles of quite reasonable wine, which went rather oddly with the eggs but gave the meal a festive air.

The long day ended with Margaret Ponting driving me to her home near the Callanish Stones, after the Count had graciously waved us off — not quite managing to conceal his relief at being shot of the monstrous, 'regiment of women'. To sum up the Count as a male chauvinist would probably be to over simplify dreadfully, but I do not think he had much use for women outside their Martha role.

It wasn't so much the notion of a bed which had tempted me to accept Margaret Ponting's offer, but the chance of having the Callanish site explained to me by an expert, for the Stone Age is something I know very little about. That night I shared a chaotic bedroom with the neatly boxed bones of a young Celtic woman who had been about 28 when she died, 3000 years before, after several pregnancies and with all her teeth intact. She might well have been still in the peat bogs of Lewis where she had been found for all she disturbed my sleep, though Margaret had half-heartedly offered to remove the bones if I found the idea of them repugnant. It's just as well I didn't mind, for I doubt there was any other corner of her house where they could have gone, even the doors to the rooms couldn't be closed for the piles of boxes and crates lying around. I don't think I could have coped in such a seemingly disorganised welter of things, domestic chaos frightens me and I have to achieve a high degree of tidiness in order not to feel threatened. My respect for Margaret increased enormously because she seemed totally unaffected by all the mess, and moved through it as though it didn't exist.

In the morning after we had repelled all the hens who had boldly tried to thrust their way into the kitchen to polish off the remains of our breakfast, we walked up to the great stone circle of Callanish. There I had the great delight of being shown a monument which previously I had valued only for its rude primitive charm and a certain eerie beauty as it loomed up out of an island mist. With Margaret Ponting's informed enthusiasm I could now see it as the rational expression of the religious beliefs of a vanished race. Under her guidance I could imagine the moon of the Spring equinox rising from behind a particular hill of Harris which (once it had been pointed out) did indeed look like the belly of a reclining pregnant woman. And as Margaret's arm traced the path of this imagined, new-born moon, and described its light casting the shadow of a particular stone up the long avenue of tall stones and into the great circle, to touch the sacred centre, I could imagine the comforting sense of eternal changelessness, mingling with the feeling of awe and mystery of creation that our ancestors must have felt here and which we largely have lost.

Not that I remember exactly what Margaret Ponting told me, her work was scientific rather than speculative and much of it was outside my range of competence. Her passion was that of the scholar and it seemed a terrible waste that she had to spend so much time scratching a living by selling bits and pieces to the all too few tourists. At the very least she should have been the official guide to the site and in a wiser society she would have a grant to enable her to devote her time purely to the research and excavations for which she is so ideally suited. But then we do not as a nation place that much value on the past and the sites which lie so thickly in these islands will safely keep their secrets into the foreseeable future, and what those vanished races were really like will continue to be a matter for speculation rather than knowledge. That we still have the monumentally important Callanish stone circle itself is little short of miraculous — a local councillor who had had a religious conversion was only a short time ago determined to get rid of the pagan relics and build a council estate on the site.

I had planned that my last few days on the islands should be spent around what is certainly my favourite bit of Lewis, if not indeed of the whole of the Outer Hebrides. It is a smaller bay to the south of Loch Roag and Gallan Head called Uig and close up against the hills of Harris. No-one who has been there when the weather is good can ever think of a more beautiful place. Although this particular August was more like April with cold gusty showers sweeping across the sea out of the south-west I was still determined to spend my last available week there.

It takes most of the day to cycle around the coast from Callanish and all along the wastes of the moorland roads there were showers followed by rainbows, like arches spanning the twisting way. After many hours in the saddle I was still only just opposite Great Bernera, on the west side and only three miles from it as the crow flies. Then the rain stopped and the evening turned fair and golden and I cycled on around the west side of Loch Roag and through the Valtos glen, which is a strange narrow depression between Gallan Head and the slopes of Suainaval, out of which one bursts suddenly upon the enormous expanse of Uig Sands. Two spurs of land slope down to enclose this perfect stretch of beach, one on each side like arms reaching out to shield it from the battering of the sea. Just a narrow entrance remains which gives on to a bay sheltered from all winds except strong north-westerlies. These are the ultimate sands of childhood, a place of endless discovery and limitless horizons.

Beyond the great spaces of Uig Sands the road meanders on for another seven miles, up and down, around headlands, past the turnings to isolated hamlets and tracks to the shore, getting narrower and less purposeful, until just beyond a slanting faded sign which reads *Tigh an Cailleach Dubh* it comes to an end altogether. The sign marks a few rickles of stones that was once a Benedictine Nunnery

'The House of the Old Black Women'. It is a strange deserted spot besides a beach called Mealista, a place of such haunting beauty and atmosphere that it is where I would build a small house if I could, and stay there. It is a place at once peaceful and yet somehow challenging, a combination that occurs not infrequently in the Outer Hebrides and is not I think purely caused by geographical features for always such sites appear to be associated with religious centres of one sort or another.

Once this coast between Mealista and Uig was thick with settlements and the hills behind sheltered countless summer shielings. The whole coast, all along the cliff tops still wears the raised weals of old lazybeds in an endless, convoluted pattern like Celtic carving, bearing witness to an extensive population. Now just a few fields are worked in the townships of Mangersta and Brenish and the last inhabited house on the road belongs to English white settlers who make a living from weaving and pottery for tourists. Not that many tourists come this far or stay the night if they do venture. Local people who had up B&B signs claimed that the tourist office in Stornoway advised visitors that there was nowhere to stay on the west coast — 'In the pay of the Stornoway Hotels they are,' claimed a local woman darkly.

Circumstances dictated my last camp ground by the heavens opening just as I was level with the cliffs above the spectacular Mangersta Sands. There was a circular enclosure on the cliff top, about fifteen feet across that looked as though it had once been an ancient dun. Only a few courses of stone were left and even these had mostly mouldered away and were grassed over, except in one section where the wall had been roughly raised to about four or five feet to afford shelter from the prevailing south-westerly wind, which was presently driving the rain hard before it. This spot had sheltered a small tent before mine as the pale scar on the grass showed. Some old folk in Mangersta who asked me in for tea later on told me that it was in Red Murdo's garden that I had camped and that there was often a small tent there as the spot seemed to attract campers, though who Red Murdo was or when he had gardened there they had no idea, it was well before their time they said and they were both over seventy. It made a good camp site and I stayed there for several days exploring the coast when there was some respite from the rain and otherwise eating and reading and finding pleasure in coping efficiently in my small space. I had never spent so many nights in a tent in any one year and now that I was acclimatised to the hard ground and to cooking and eating in a prone position I was finding that I quite enjoyed it. The rare nights when I slept for seven hours or so without once waking seemed a triumph. I made a candle holder out of any empty bean can and this gave me a quite disproportionate sense of achievement — I was digging in, home-making.

My surroundings were spectacular in the extreme. Below me and inland, huge waves rolled in to thunder and break upon Mangersta Beach with an uninterrupted force and grandeur I had not seen elsewhere up here; normally such fury expended itself against the cliffs or on the boulder-strewn storm beaches and the sandy bays were more sheltered places. Directly before the tent's opening and at no great distance from it, the land fell away to the edge of the sheer headland, in front of which were slender stacks like huge needles in a giant's pincushion. There was a way to scramble down to the sea and wander about in the sheltered shingle coves at the feet of these stacks. It was from there that the older inhabitants of Mangersta could remember launching their twenty foot, open fishing boats and sailing out over the Atlantic on still summer nights, beyond the sight of land.

There was no still weather at all while I was there. I'd wriggle out of the tent in a brief dry spell and my wet clothes, soaked by the last shower would be wind dried in minutes, as I made my way across the tops of the cliffs, concentrating on keeping my balance and not being blown over the edge. The ground I walked on was covered with a close-growing vivid green weed that looked from a distance like the finest bowling green turf. Another bullying herring gull, suspecting that I had designs upon his territory added to the excitement by stalking me and suddenly flying close, his harsh cries echoing around the rocks.

One day when I was walking on Uig Sands I met a group of youths who were camping there and canoeing. They were bright boys mostly in their last year at the prestigious Stornoway secondary school and one was in his final year at University. They asked me in for a cup of coffee and having run out of meths, in the true island style of making do, they managed to prime their stove with bits of fluff pulled from a towel. We talked while a minor gale raged outside their roomy but leaky kitchen tent and I asked them what they thought their futures were likely to be. Of the ten there only two thought they would stay on Lewis, the rest were quite resigned to leaving the islands. One of the two was the undergraduate and he said that after two years away he knew that he had to live on Lewis no matter what work he did as it was the only place he wanted to live.

When I asked them what was the worst element of life on Lewis as far as they were concerned, I was surprised that they unanimously plumped for religion. I was even more surprised that it was not the restrictions of religious observation that they found so galling but the hypocrisy of it all. Sundays they painted as a day of constant fret and niggling, with parental injunctions to turn radios down and come away from windows to avoid neighbours seeing or hearing them do what they ought not to be doing, and that comprised anything at all other than reading the Bible. They were quite insistent about it — it was not the deed itself but other people seeing it that made it heinous — pure hypocrisy they said with all the absolute conviction of youth. Pressed further they admitted that it must be a genuine belief for some people but they still insisted that for the majority religion was simply social pressure, fear of what your neighbours thought in a place where neighbours were so important to life. You had to conform they said otherwise life was made unbearable for you. The youth who was planning to stay said that he too would be forced to go through the motions of conforming and he would do so even though the thought made him angry, because you cannot live on an island if your neighbours ostracise you.

There was currently a religious revival they told me and people were becoming 'converted' even at school but it seemed to them that this was largely play-acting or at best, hysteria. Life in Lewis was dominated by the Free Church they said and its people were in all the positions of power; particularly in the schools, where they claimed indoctrination was in operation from the first class onwards. If they felt so bitterly about it all, why didn't they openly rebel? I wondered and their response to that was that they couldn't possibly because it would rebound upon their parents. I think that reply showed me more about the social cohesion of the islands, its strengths and its weaknesses than anything else I saw or heard there.

Towards the end of that last week there came a day when quite suddenly I craved comfort and had had enough of wet clothes, cramped quarters and hard ground. I had anticipated this and had my plans ready to move into a guest house I had heard of which overlooked Uig Sands and sounded like the exact antithesis to the rough self-sufficiency of the previous months. *Baile na Cille* it was called and was yet another ex-manse, one with a sad history for the last incumbent had hanged himself there. He'd been cooking the books for ages, claiming that he had a healthy, flourishing congregation at a time when every Parish Church on the Protestant islands was virtually empty, the folk having deserted *en masse* to the Free Church, and every Parish Church minister was sick with anxiety because they were paid by results. In reality his only member was his housekeeper who couldn't desert for obvious reasons and when the Establishment in Edinburgh, eager to learn how he had succeeded where every one else had failed informed him of their impending visit, he couldn't face the shame of exposure.

I had been told about the guesthouse by the Vaughans at Ness and in fact their lovely busy painting of the cricket match had been commisioned by the owners, Richard and Joanna Gollin. I found it a place where the term 'no expense spared' meant a quiet solid comfort, rather than brash ostentation. The Gollins are young and have succeeded in what they set out to do in a relatively short time. Both come from the home counties and both visited the Outer Hebrides when they were still at school and decided then that it was where they wanted to live. A judicious claiming of available grants and a great deal of hard work have provided them with a splendid home and business. The 18th century manse has been improved and refurbished to a standard of affluent comfort — good taste without too much individualism. At £24 a night for dinner bed and breakfast it offered tremendous value, for the food was excellent and plentiful, the rooms were attractive and the site, overlooking the full sweep of the sands was superb. I was lucky to get in because with so few places to stay on this lovely coast it was quite full, but the Gollins kindly allowed me to take over their small daughter's room at a reduced rate and in return I showed them how to rig the sailing dinghy they had just purchased. The Gollins have two young children and Richard also has a teaching job in Stornoway. They work tremendously hard for very long hours during their short season and then take their own holidays in winter when there are no guests.

While I was there a young German whom the Gollins had met on the Continent the previous year, arrived with his tent. He had been intrigued by what they had told him about their island life and had decided to come and camp in their grounds and see it for himself. He was a highly intelligent, rather waspish youth with his attitudes to life neatly worked out — 'Typical English food is fish and chips, marmalade and baked beans.' As a result his instant surrender to the spell of the Outer Hebrides was all the more surprising. The first night we all went for a moonlight walk in a rare spell of milder weather and before we had gone a mile along the marvellous empty sands, beside a sea that was full of soft murmurings and silver shadows, he was declaring that he had found Paradise and would travel no further, for what was the point when perfection was there within his grasp?

I'm glad his visit had coincided with mine, for his unequivocal response reminded me of what I had felt when I had first come out here. It seems to me that he was clearly stating what this string of 'precious fragments' was really all about. It is 'Paradise' to individuals who want what it has to offer and don't mind doing without many of the modern trappings which modern Western man thinks are essential to life. It is one of the few places left in Britain where an individual can choose to live differently in a habitat where nature is still the most dominant presence. I'd come expecting to find something else — an older culture, a communal way of life with a social structure strong enough to withstand alien pressures, something precious preserved over the centuries. I didn't find that, which is not to say that it doesn't still exist in a few small pockets. For me the old life style seemed on its last legs with people paying lip service to past values and ideas, while taking on all the expectations of the modern consumer society and it seemed to be the alien values that had won. I heard lots of talk about a valuable cultural heritage, but I saw glimpses of it only amongst the few and those mostly the oldest of the population. Television soap operas were as much the daily cultural fare as anywhere else in the country and the Gaelic language seemed to be disappearing fast. Nor had subsidies prevented much of the land falling into disuse, lending such an air of desolation and neglect to the landscape.

I was often told of what 'the government' ought to be doing for the islands — creating work so as to halt the population erosion. While I sympathise with anyone out of work, particularly the young, I don't think it's the 'government's' job to keep people anywhere, nor can they do so except in prisons and if it is 'government's' job to create work then there is the rest of Britain to consider too and the numbers in all the Outer Hebrides are just a drop in the ocean of unemployment.

Terrible injustices have been perpetrated on the people of the Outer Hebrides; the last two hundred years of their unenviable history is as black a period as any. It is small wonder that so many of them have looked elsewhere for a more satisfactory life or that children raised on stories of such inequalities should seek their future away from the islands. Something very precious has indeed been destroyed. But it is not only the people who have suffered, the islands themselves have been exhausted under a regime that put profit first and destroyed much of the fertility of the soil. It didn't seem to me that subsidies were doing much to reverse these centuries of misuse. I read in one modern sociological treatise that the people don't really feel the land belongs to them yet and this was why they were not prepared to effect real, long-term improvements. If they really feel that way will they, I wonder, be able to resist pressures to turn the place into a nuclear dumping ground or an advanced missile base or a testing ground for chemical warfare?

What gave me most hope for the future of the Outer Hebrides were the individuals who had chosen to live there. Whether 'white settlers' or returned natives, they were the ones who had made a rational choice between different value systems and decided that they would be richer in their own terms, living there than anywhere else. Where people make that sort of commitment, a level of caring ensues which is seldom matched by people who simply find themselves in situations. Such people have a clear idea of what the islands give them — which is of course the sum of what they themselves give to the islands.

I was thinking of the people I'd met out there as I steamed back across the Minch, past the Summer Isles to Ullapool. Many of them would I suppose be considered 'dropouts' in some societies, because they are so unambitious in worldly terms. I thought of Jack and Polly in the manse garden on Barra; Chris Spears in the house he'd made out of a byre on the edge of Berneray; the Vaughans; Margaret Ponting with her passion for prehistory; the Miles, the Gollins, and the man whose name I've forgotten, who'd come back to his small village near the island of Scarp. I see these people as the new inheritors, upon whom the rest of us have to depend to preserve this fragile chain of precious islands.